FERRYPORT ADVENTURES: RETURN OF THE FEY ADVENTURE PATH, PART 2

THE DEAD GULCH

A World of Uteria, Pathfinder Roleplaying Game Compatible Adventure Module

CREDITS:

Authors: Michael Bielaczyc, Shonn Everett, and Cameron Tomele
Editors: Dane Clark Collins and D.C. Fontana
Cover Artist: Melissa Gay
Interior Artists: A.L. Ashbaugh, Michael Bielaczyc, Paul Bielaczyc, Christopher Burdett, Sam Flegal, Melissa Gay, Dennis Skotak, and Robert Skotak
Interior Design: Loraine Flegal

Copyright 2015, Lone Wanderer Entertainment

TABLE OF CONTENTS

THE DEAD GULCH ADVENTURE

INTRODUCTION 4

PRELUDE 7

STARTING THE ADVENTURE 8

THE RESLY MANOR 10

THE CIRCUS 12

THE TODAREN FAMILY CIRCUS AND FESTIVAL! 15

THE TOMB OF THE RESLYS 32

BACK TO THE CIRCUS 39

THE DEAD GULCH 42

AFTER THE ADVENTURE 55

PREGENERATED ADVENTURERS 56

GLOSSARY OF PEOPLE AND PLACES 66

THE TOME OF THE ARTS 69

THE HISTORY OF MAGIC 72

GROUPS OF MAGIC USERS 73

THE MAGIC OF UTERIA 76

SPELLCASTING CLASSES 80

SPELLS OF UTERIA 88

THE DEAD GULCH

INTRODUCTION

The Dead Gulch (FA02) is a Pathfinder Roleplaying Game compatible adventure designed for 4 to 6 characters of 2nd level. Characters will advance an average of two levels by completing this module, depending upon how well they are able to overcome the challenges and dark creatures that block their path.

This adventure is part 2 of the Ferryport Adventures *Return of the Fey* adventure path, set in the World of Uteria, which was introduced in *The Elves of Uteria* sourcebook.[1] The first Uteria module in this adventure path, *The Goblins of Kaelnor Forest* (FA01),[2] includes *The Wanderer's Guide to Ferryport*. Though not necessary, it would be best if the players experienced FA01 prior to playing FA02, to introduce them to Uteria and its unique twist on magic use. New modules in this adventure path will be published by Lone Wanderer Entertainment several times per year, and will see the players become some of the most skilled and respected heroes in Uteria by its end.

Your group will need the Pathfinder Roleplaying Game core books to make use of this adventure. It is also highly recommended you have *The Elves of Uteria* sourcebook as well as FA01, *The Goblins of Kaelnor Forest* (which includes *The Wanderer's Guide to Ferryport*, containing background information on major characters in Ferryport and maps of the city and key establishments).

Several pre-generated characters have been provided at the end of this booklet. The Story Guide (called the SG from here on) may find these useful if the players do not wish to spend the time to roll up characters or if the players are new to Pathfinder and the SG wants to encourage them to jump straight into play. In addition, if there are not enough players, or they lack a specific character class in their party that the SG thinks they should have, the SG can use one or more of the pre-generated characters as non-player characters.

This adventure can easily be adapted to fit in any fantasy RPG setting, if the SG does not wish to adopt the World of Uteria setting, but will fit most readily in a "low fantasy" setting, where the inhabitants have not had much exposure to magic or non-human characters.

[1] *The Elves of Uteria* World of Uteria sourcebook by Lone Wander Entertainment, is available on Paizo's website at http://paizo.com/products/btpy9bbr?The-Elves-of-Uteria

[2] *The Goblins of Kaelnor Forest* (FA01) and *The Wanderer's Guide to Ferryport* by Lone Wander Entertainment, is available on Paizo's website at http://paizo.com/products/btpy9bla?The-Ferryport-Adventures-The-Goblins-of-Kaelnor-Forest

OUTSIDE THE CITY

A cool wind blew against the stained gray stone of the Ferryport wall.

A man leaned against the wall, a short wooden pipe in his hand. A spark from a whetstone, and the tobac inside the pipe, started to glow orange. A few wisps of smoke escaped the man's lips as he peered across the wet field. Large tents were being erected; people ran to and fro; shouts filled the quickly darkening evening. His eyes narrowed as he watched a small group who walked among the busy people, pointing and shouting their own instructions.

He shuffled a bit, his long weather-stained coat scratching against the wall as he shifted more of his weight against it.

A voice from behind him broke his concentration. "Well now, I didn't expect to find you so close to civilization, Aldulf."

The first man took a long drag from his pipe and turned slowly. Smoke came out of his mouth as he flashed a lopsided smile. "Well now, I didn't think the Tower would let you out these days. What are you doing in this strange and distant land, Malynn?"

The speaker was a man of average height, his clothes finer than Aldulf's, but showing a little wear around the edges. Behind him stood a tall bald man, his face stern and impassive. Both newcomers stared at Aldulf with contemplation, but then Malynn returned the smile. "Same as you, business for the Tower, though I go about mine in a different manner." His eyes strayed down to the small crossbow hanging from Aldulf's belt. " I heard you were about, though someone said you were sniffing around the swamps to the west."

Aldulf leaned completely back on the wall and took another puff of his pipe. " Chasing some silly village superstitions of witches. It was nothing more than a mother-daughter with a smattering of power. They aren't doing anything dark with it, just telling fortunes and taking coin."

Malynn's eyebrow raised. "That doesn't sound like the Aldulf I know, letting some wylders walk around free? There was a time when you would have had them in chains being dragged to the Tower to be silenced."

"The Tower is far way from here. And the world isn't what it used to be." Aldulf emptied the still smoldering ashes from the pipe. " I guess you're here to pull rank and tell me to leave the circus be?"

Malynn walked forward and surveyed the tents and people in the distant field. "There is plenty in the city to keep you busy. Go find some wylder cutting up rats in the sewers and drag him into the daylight. There is no use for a heavy hand here."

Aldulf walked behind the shorter man, not looking in his direction. He patted the silent bald man on the shoulder, "Keep him out of trouble — I don't think he is ready for this new world outside the Tower."

As Aldulf started the long walk back to the South Gate, the cloudy sky opened up and began to rain once again.

Illustration by Michael Bielaczyc

ADVENTURE SYNOPSIS

Plagues have ravaged the lands for generations. While the city of Ferryport has been spared the worst, it has still seen its fair share of death and pestilence. During the worst outbreaks, corpses lined the streets and the people had to find a place to dispose of the bodies. In the northern city, they blocked the sewers and filled them like catacombs with the charred bones of the dead. In the southern parts of the city, they dumped the corpses by the thousands into the canyons which split the land between South Hollow and Lyncast.

The adventurers are hired by Tain Northbow, a druid and advisor to Silas Monta, one of the most powerful men in Ferryport. A man of his power and influence he has many friends and many enemies. One of Silas's longtime adversaries among the Guildmasters is Taris Resly, or Lord Resly, as he prefers to be called. After the treason of Lord Glycyn, former ruler of Ferryport, Resly opposed all motions to move toward a democratic government. Resly believed the city needed a single strong-handed ruler, supported by the guild masters, who would in turn become minor lords in the city.

Now, Resly has been missing for over two weeks. The City Guard have investigated, but have found no trace of Resly, save a rumored visit to a traveling circus. His house sits abandoned and watched over by the Guard. Rumors have started to flutter about that Silas may have eliminated his biggest opponent.

To clear his name, Silas asked Tain to find an outside group to look into the disappearance and report back with anything they find. The adventurers, who have been doing odd jobs for Guardsman Garamond, are asked to meet Tain at the Southgate Inn. He wants to discuss a possible job for our young adventurers.

STORY GUIDE'S INFORMATION

Lord Resly has not disappeared; he has just gone underground due to circumstances outside the current power struggle in Ferryport. Resly is gifted in magic. He learned many years ago that he had strange abilities,

but it wasn't until an envoy from Jaeldor visited him that he began to learn his true power. Belial Fue'vuer saw the potential in Resly and began secretly training him in ravaging magic[3]. Three weeks ago, his wife discovered him deep within his own wine cellars practicing the dark arts. He tried in vain to explain his gift to her, but she was appalled and fled. He chased her up the stairs and a struggle ensued. Lady Resly tore loose from her husband and fell down the stone stairs. When Resly came to his senses and reached her, she lay dead with a broken neck. He spent the next weeks trying to find a way to being her back from the afterlife.

Luckily for Resly, the circus had returned to town. There, a powerful sage named Rosaga helped him find the correct incantations and ritual to revive his dead wife. But Rosaga had her own dark motives for helping Resly. At his family grave, with the help of Rosaga, he raised what he thought was his deceased wife. Unbeknownst to him, Rosaga used his desires to summon a powerful entity from the Navirim, or dream world, that had long looked to break into this world.

The adventurers travel to the circus, Lord Resly's manor, and finally his family grave to uncover his whereabouts. After the fight with Lord Resly, the spirit possessing his wife's body escapes. Tracking it back to the circus, they find Rosaga has begun a ritual to summon the spirit of her dead love from the Navirim. After she is stopped and the locals set at ease, Malynn the wizard sends the players to the West to destroy the spirit which Rosaga and Resly brought over. After journeying deep into the Dead Gulch, the adventurers confront the Sirin, and finally defeat her.

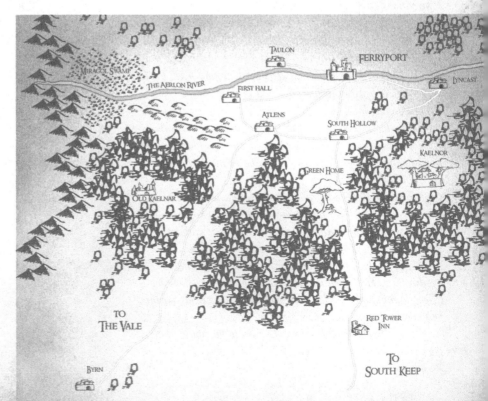

---

[3]   For more on Ravaging, see the *Tome of the Arts: The Magic of Uteria*

PRELUDE

At the end of *The Goblins of Kaelnor Forest* (FA01), the adventurers should have been sent to the city of Ferryport with a letter of introduction from the guard in South Hollow to give to a Ferryport city guardsman named Garamond. The letter explained that they had provided valuable services for the town of South Hollow and could be trusted to provide services for Ferryport as well, if their talents were needed. Since that time some weeks past, Garamond has contacted the party to perform a few small tasks for the guard.

The adventure begins on one of the roads that leads into Ferryport, with our heros fighting a band of highway robbers Garamond hired them to track down. Disguised as traders, he loaned them a wagon and a retired old city guard horse named Goliath to complete their disguise. The job was to subdue the bandits and bring them in alive to stand trial, not kill them. The bandits are not very tough, just bullies who have been relying mostly on bravado and intimidation.

BANDITS (4)   CR 1/2
XP 200 each
Male human fighter 1
CN Medium humanoid (human)
Init +1
Senses Perception +1

DEFENSE
AC 11, touch 11, flat-footed 10 (+1 Dex)
hp 8 (1d10+3)
Fort +4, Ref +3, Will +3

OFFENSE
Speed 30 ft.

STATISTICS
STR 15, DEX 13, CON 14, INT 11, WIS 13, CHA 11
Languages Common
Feats Iron Will, Lightning Reflexes, Weapon Focus (Longsword)
Special Qualities Bonus Feat, Bonus Feats, Skilled

SPECIAL ABILITIES
   Bonus Feat Humans select one extra feat at 1st level.
   Bonus Feats At 1st level, and at every even level thereafter, a fighter gains a bonus feat in addition to those gained from normal advancement (meaning that the fighter gains a feat at every level). These bonus feats must be selected from those listed as combat feats, sometimes also called "fighter bonus feats." Upon reaching 4th level, and every four levels thereafter (8th, 12th, and so on), a fighter can choose to learn a new bonus feat in place of a bonus feat he has already learned. In effect, the fighter loses the bonus feat in exchange for the new one. The old feat cannot be one that was used as a prerequisite for another feat, prestige class, or other ability. A fighter can only change one feat at any given level and must choose whether or not to swap the feat at the time he gains a new bonus feat for the level.
   Skilled Humans gain an additional skill rank at first level and one additional rank whenever they gain a level.

After capturing the bandits, the adventurers haul them in to the city guard; and their contact, Garamond, meets with them, paying them 20 sp each for their service. The goal of this brief encounter is to give the players some fighting to get their adrenaline going right off the bat, get them to Garamond so he can give them their next assignment, and get a few coins in their pockets.

As they enter the town with their cart full of bandits, read the following:

As you lead your cart full of bandits into the city, you suddenly see a man walking through the streets, his head high above the crowd, wearing brightly colored clothing and juggling several burning torches in the air. Behind him walks a huge muscular man, holding a metal A-frame construction upon his shoulders. Above his head on the metal poles is a beautiful young woman, hanging from them, spinning and swinging, and flying up on top to balance and walk the short length of the top beam, all while the strong man holds her up and walks calmly down the street. Behind them, you see a dark haired man in a bright costume walking along, putting up printed flyers here and there, barking out that this is the final week of the Circus here at Ferryport before they move on.

STARTING THE ADVENTURE

After paying the party for their services to the city, guardsman Garamond tells them he recommended them to the druid, Tain Northbow, for a new job and directs them to the Southgate Inn. He says Tain will be looking for them to meet him the next morning just after sunup for breakfast. This gives the party the rest of the day and evening to rest, purchase supplies they may need with their newfound money, and get to know a bit more about Ferryport. The SG should feel free to let them wander about the town, if they have not already done so, and give them a taste for the setting based on the information in *The Wanderer's Guide to Ferryport* (included in FA01).

If asked, Garamond can describe what Tain looks like (see below) and will tell them Tain is a highly trusted member of the Druid Council. It is a great honor to be asked to perform a service for him, perhaps much more valuable than any money they might earn from the job.

SOUTHGATE INN

When the adventurers arrive at Southgate Inn the following morning, read the following:

The Southgate Inn is busy. All the tables are full, and people stand shoulder-to-shoulder in the common room. A minstrel tells stories in the corner, but you have little mind to pay attention. Weeks ago, you were sent by Guard Buerger to the city proper with a letter of recommendation. You earned some silver doing odd jobs for the contacts you made within the guard, but now you have been asked to the inn by none other that Tain Northbow, the personal counsel of Silas Monta, one of the most influential men in the city. *

While all other tables are full, you find one empty with a small red rock sitting in the middle of it. At the head of the table sits a tall man, his blond beard and hair marking him from the north. His leather and fur cloak are tossed over the back of the tall chair he sits in. Though he looks to have seen about 30 cycles, his face is tanned and weather worn. While there is nothing menacing about this man, he radiates power and commands your attention.

Tain is tall and powerfully built. He is easy to smile and comforting to those who speak with him, his deep voice soothing. He is honest with the adventurers and will answer most questions that they ask. It is known that he is part of the Druid Council, and any magic user who asks would be directed to privately talk to him.**

As for the job, his proposal is simple, each adventurer receives 10 sp per day while investigating the disappearance of Lord Resly. He suggests that a good place to start in the search for Resly is the circus outside the city. It is a yearly attraction, and Tain doesn't suspect them of foul play; but it is rumored that it was the last place Lord Resly was seen.

* The adventurers each have an extra 20 sp from the odd jobs they have performed since the first adventure.

*** Tain is a member of the Druids and a magic user. He does not flaunt this or press his beliefs on those around him. His closeness with Silas Monta affords him some protection from the prejudices against the Druids and others associated with the arts. If any player is interested, Tain is capable and willing to take them under his wing and train them as a druidic luminari as described in the **Tome of the Arts: The Magic of Uteria**, which is included at the back of this adventure. He will begin their training right away, so any Wylder interested in advancing as a Luminar must wait until after this adventure.*

Knowledge that Tain may impart to the adventurers

Tain has been part of the politics of Ferryport for quite some time, so he can inform them on much of the information found in the *Guide of Ferryport* book. How much is up to the Story Guide.

Other Information

- *I do not believe Lord Resly is a bad man; but he lost much power and influence with the imprisoning of Filac Glycyn, former ruler of Ferryport.*
- *After the treason of Lord Glycyn, former ruler of Ferryport, Lord Resly directly opposed Silas Monta's referendum to democratize Ferryport. He wanted another to sit on the throne of Rivenhall Castle.*
- *Resly believed the city needed a single strong-handed ruler, supported by the guild masters, who in turn, would become minor lords in the city.*
- *Due to the enmity between the two men, some are suggesting Silas is behind Resly's disappearance. This is why Silas asked me to find an outside group to investigate and hopefully clear his name.*
- *The guard questioned Resly's servants, and they claimed that Lady Resly had disappeared before her husband did. One said he heard a heated argument before she disappeared.*

- *Resly has always been a patron of the circus for as far back as anyone can remember, so it is not out of the ordinary that he would attend the traveling show; but it does appear to be the last place he was seen.*
- *The circus is located just south of the city beyond South Gate. The tents and outdoor shows open just past midday, and the festivities run until almost midnight.*

When the adventurers are ready to take their leave, Tain offers them a small pouch containing 8 goodberries[4]. He explains that they should eat one or more berries if they are injured and they will provide a very small amount of healing. He says the berries will stay fresh for a few days and will also provide the sustenance of an entire meal if needed. (They heal 1 hit point per berry, which can make the difference between life and death for low level characters).

TWO PATHS
The players have been informed about the Circus, but may also wish to investigate Resley's Manor. Allow them to pursue whichever avenue they wish, as both paths point to each other and his current residence in his family tomb.

Illustration by Michael Bielaczyc

---

[4] See Pathfinder Core Rulebook spell Goodberry

THE RESLY MANOR

Lord Resly's Estate is a three-story building behind high stone fences. It sits across the street from the southern wall of Ferryport and the Sanctum of the Gods temple. Even though it is a beautiful mansion, it looks to have fallen into a little disrepair. Dead trees poke up above the walls, and the house color is gray and peeling. An iron gate stands closed ahead of you, a large rusted lock holding it shut.

There is no evidence of anyone in the house. The lock is easy enough to pick, a DC of 16, or the stone wall easy to climb, DC 18. The adventurers should be allowed to roam the house, but the house has been ransacked for valuables (by Resly looking to fund the resurrection of his wife). Resly has also moved most of his books to his graveyard laboratory or traded them with Rosaga for payment. There are a few clues left, but most of the house is just filled with non-valuable or mundane items.

The house is ornately decorated on the inside, but everything has a coating of dust or looks a little worn. Dark spots on the wall show where paintings once hung, dead flowers are spilled out on the floor — their vases gone, boxes and chests opened or flipped over. Everything in the manor looks as if it has been rummaged through or taken.

In the large kitchen, a door with a very large chain and padlock stands wide open, the chain and lock dangling from the door handle. A long set of steep stair steps leads down into the darkness. A still cold emanates from the depths, carrying a slight scent of cedar. (Resly had no need to lock it after he removed all his belongings.)

The stairs lead down perhaps 20 or more feet and open into a 15' x 20' room, with wine racks standing against the two long walls. This is obviously Resly's wine cellar, buried deep in the earth to provide a natural cool temperature for the wines. The walls of the cellar are made of cedar planks. You immediately notice there is a thick layer of dust on the floor and many tracks in and out, overlaying each other many times.

CLUES

Perception Check:
- DC 3 — Just about anyone who looks can easily tell that all the tracks seem to be from the same set of boots, which appear, from the size and shape, to be a man's boots.
- DC 5 — A door, which looks like it would blend in with the cellar wall, is left open and a dark chamber beyond stands completely empty. Maybe it was some sort of safe room or secret

study. The tracks lead in and out of this small room many times.
- DC 15 — Large sections of books are missing from the study. Some were moved to the graveyard laboratory, others sold, and the most valuable were traded to Rosaga.
- DC 20 — Under the wine rack in the cellar is a bit of parchment that gives strange ingredients. It has the name "Gertras" scribbled at the bottom.
- DC 15 — Local Knowledge to know that Gertras is a shop owner in the merchant district.
- DC 25 — Under the lip of some of the stairs, there is dried blood.
- DC 30 — Someone with really good tracking skills may notice a single set of footprints from female dress shoes underneath the many layers of men's boot prints, and can tell from her gait that she was running for the stairs.

As the adventurers are wrapping up their visit to the basement, they hear the door open and footsteps. It is Belial Fue'vuer coming to see if his friend has returned. At this point, Belial does not know where Resly is; and his investigation into the circus has turned up nothing. A haughty Jaeldorian nobleman accompanied by guards does not loosen any tongues in a traveling show. If he finds the players, read the following:

A skinny man, his stooped posture making him look hunched, sneers at you. A slight bit of grey touches the temples of his dark hair under a feather-laden hat. His clothing marks him as nobility of some sort, and the three guards with him all wear the same lion crest on their blue tabards. The skinny man places his hand on the hilt of a thin sword at his side. "Well, now, what rabble do we have here, skulking like rats in my friend's cellar?"

He may threaten the adventurers, but he will not arrest them or call the city guards. He does not want to draw attention to Resly's disappearance or himself in this matter. But he does want to find his friend. Fue'vuer will ask the following questions:
- Who are you, and what are you doing in my Lord's manor?
- Who gave you permission to have anything to do with this household and its people?
- What do you know of Resly? Some say he is off vacationing in the South, but that does not ring true.
- Have you been to that wretched circus? Those heathens would not speak to me of my friend, though I know he was a frequent visitor. If so, what did you learn?

Illustration by Michael Bielaczyc

Belial sees the adventurers as possible scapegoats if things go badly with Resly, or as potentially useful for his plans in the future. He will not push them too hard. Instead, he is interested in what they say and will then let them go. Belial is aware of Rosaga and her power; he doesn't care for her. He feels that she is power hungry and she had something to do with the loss of his influential friend. He will point the adventurers back toward the circus and specifically Rosaga.

GERTRAS' HERBS

Gertras' shop is in the merchant district. If the players go looking for her to question her, pretty much anyone in the district can point them to her shop, Gertras' Herbs. She specializes in poultices, herbs, and remedies.

When the players enter her shop, read the following:

As you enter the shop, you see all manner of drying herbs and poultices around the cluttered shop; and a multitude of smells accosts your noses, most of them quite foul. An old grey-haired woman approaches you, using a gnarled walking stick to support her. "Good day, my lords and ladies. How may Gertras be of assistance today?"

If questioned, or shown the slip of paper, she will pretend not to remember, as she comments on how they look to be adventurers and offers them a healing ointment for 5 sp. If the players catch on and purchase her concoction, she will suddenly remember Resly's visit, and tell them that Lord Resly spent a king's fortune for some very rare items and ingredients. She adds that just yesterday, two young women came in and bought out the rest of her stock of those same items. The younger one called the older one "Oh-lee-sa" or something like that.

The healing ointment will actually heal 1d8 hit points if rubbed on a wound. Half the ointment can be rubbed on a minor wound to heal 1d4, and can thus last for two applications.

THE CIRCUS

ON THE ROAD TO THE CIRCUS

Play this encounter if the adventurers set out for the circus in the late evening or after dark. If they go earlier in the day and find themselves returning to town after dark, then delay the encounter till then.

Early in their experiments, Resly and Rosaga killed and tried to reanimate one of the Boggarts. They thought it had not worked and dumped the body in the gulch, but it was just slow in reanimating. It later awoke and has been wandering around, looking for something to eat for days.

Read the following, based on whether the adventurers are heading for or leaving from the circus:

Heading to the circus at night

As you walk along what is quickly becoming a well-trodden path leaving Southgate across the fields to the circus, you can see the bright lights of torches and exotic paper lanterns lighting up the night sky over the circus. The tents are lit up from the inside, glowing in eerie shades of yellow, red, and orange, like gargantuan jack-o-lanterns.

The myriad sounds of the city begin to fade into nothingness behind you when you have put a couple hundred paces between you and the city walls, and you can just make out the faint sounds of high-pitched laughter and merriment coming from the circus.

Heading back to town at night

As you walk along what is quickly becoming a well-trodden path between the circus and the city, the big torch and lantern lit tents glow in eerie shades of yellow, red, and orange, like gargantuan jack-o-lanterns, casting eerie flickering lights and shadows across the grassy fields.

The high-pitched sounds of laughter and merriment fade into silence behind you when you have put a couple hundred paces between you and the circus; and you can just make out the faint sounds of late night activity coming from the city ahead, most of it probably coming from the Southgate Inn.

Read the following for either situation

You suddenly hear what you could swear is a faint moan from nearby off the side of the path in the field. The flickering lights from the circus in the night sky make it difficult to see, even for those with enhanced night vision; but you can just make out a shadowy figure lying in the grass about twenty paces from you. With a painful high-pitched groan, as if injured and in pain, the figure pulls itself up and stands upright. For a moment, it

appears to be an injured child, standing about three feet in height and dressed only in dark tattered rags, but as it turns toward you, the flickering lights of the circus suddenly light its face, and you see a ghoulish pale visage like that of a corpse, staring at you with white, unblinking eyes the size of apples, that remind you of dead fish's eyes. It lets out a gurgling moan and raising one rotting little hand toward you, and begins to move in your direction, its mouth gaping open with spittle drooling down its chin.

ZOMBIE, BOGGART (1)   CR 1/2
XP 200
NE Medium undead
Init +0
Senses Darkvision 60 ft., Perception +0

DEFENSE
AC 12, touch 10, flat-footed 12 (+2 natural)
hp 12 (2d8+3)
Fort +0, Ref +0, Will +3
DR 5/slashing
Immune Undead Traits

OFFENSE
Speed 30 ft.
Melee Slam +4 (1d6+4)

STATISTICS
STR 17, DEX 10, CON —, INT —, WIS 10, CHA 10
Base Atk +1; **CMB** +4; **CMD** 14
Feats Toughness
Special Qualities Staggered

SPECIAL ABILITIES
Staggered (Ex) The adventurers will most likely easily dispatch it, but will get their adrenaline going right off the bat and plant the seeds of suspicion to start growing. If they try to track it, they will have much difficulty, as it is dark. In the event they have an exceptional tracker and make a DC of 25 for tracking in the grassy field at night, they will discover it has been lying here for some time and before that wandered aimlessly around in the dark. It they spend a lot of time tracking it, have them encounter 2 more boggart zombies with the same stats. These lie in wait in the grass and reach out to grab them as they pass (surprise situation).

ZB	1	16	√	8
X	10	15	√	
MA	3	7	√	
G	19	2		
M	17	9	√	

Illustration by Melissa Gay

ZOMBIES, BOGGARTS (2)   CR 1/2
XP 200 each
(same stats as Boggart Zombie, page 12)

If they are persistent enough and roll another DC 25 for tracking, they can discover the zombies seemed to come from the gulch. They will not be able to find any tracks leading to the graveyard because their bodies were thrown from the cliff above into the gulch, so there are no tracks to follow there.

At the SG's discretion, Malynn and Lorthain may witness the adventurers fighting the zombies from a distance. If any of them casts any visible spells, Malynn will know they have a spell caster, but he will also know that they seem to be using their powers for good.

THE CIRCUS

Outside the South Gate, a huddle of large striped tents can be seen in the now flattened fields. The prairie grass that had grown there just months ago has now been trampled into the mud by visitors from the city who have come day and night for the festivities. The circus has always stayed a month, always at the end of spring, as far back as anyone in Ferryport can remember. Unlike most sideshows and traveling attractions, this is known as "The Circus of Ferryport" to the city's residents, even though it is actually named the Todaren Family Circus. It is different from other traveling shows in that it has a theme, one of reliving the past age, before the plagues and twisting, when magic filled the air and legends were born.

When the players enter the circus, read the following:

Your boots are caked with mud, but you hardly notice. All around you, the sounds and sights of the circus attract your attention. Barkers shout to passersby, luring them into tents for a show of whip cracking or another tent to see a fey pony, captured from the Never* itself! A tall man passes by on giant stilts, smiling and passing out free tickets for a taste of "dwarven mead" available at the makeshift tavern. Citizens of Ferryport walk by, some eating the decadent foods of the festival, others dressed in all manner of costumes and wardrobe. Oil lamps light the way, flickering through colored glass to give an otherworldly appearance to everything around you.

* *The Never is the common word for the Navirim, the "dream world" that is a source for magic and many of the dark creatures that now invade Uteria.*

13

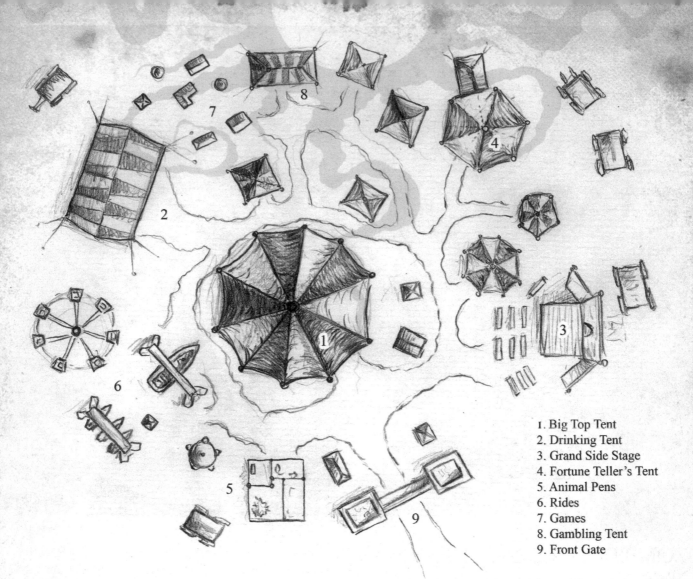

1. Big Top Tent
2. Drinking Tent
3. Grand Side Stage
4. Fortune Teller's Tent
5. Animal Pens
6. Rides
7. Games
8. Gambling Tent
9. Front Gate

The Story Guide may play the circus as he sees fit. Below are some of the key characters who travel with the festival and who may provide clues to the adventurers. You can also have them enter tents, watch shows, and generally take in the whole circus. Below the characters are some key interactions and some optional encounters.

The players can start to suspect Rosaga, but if they try anything beyond questioning her, Cameron and the others of the circus will intervene. The adventurers are to find Resly, not interfere with the circus at this point. The goal is for them to suspect that something more sinister is happening, but to be pointed toward the graveyard as the last place that Resly was seen.

Key Encounters
- Cameron notices them asking around and pulls them to the side.
- Malynn notices them and sends them an invitation to meet at the Southgate Inn in the city after.
- Rosaga's Tent — Rosaga's oldest daughter will talk to the adventurers and point them away from their family.

- Oleysa (Last) — Oleysa followed Resly because she didn't like him. The past couple of weeks, he would come to her mother's tent and then leave carrying a bag full of stuff. She followed him one night to the edge of the massive graveyard to the East.

Optional Encounters
The following encounters are detailed in the section titled "Optional Encounters" immediately after the circus encounter and NPC descriptions. If the PCs spend a great deal of time in the circus questioning its proprietor and workers, the SG may want to break up the investigation and role playing with these encounters to give the players some action.
- Drunken Brawl
- The Loose Thundrom (an escaped circus beast endangers the patrons)
- Pickpocket
- Malynn and Lorthain

THE TODAREN FAMILY CIRCUS AND FESTIVAL!

CAMERON TODAREN
Ringmaster

Cameron's dark brown hair is cut short and kept close to his head, sideburns pointing like arrows to his cheekbones and a small triangular goatee that is in constant motion as he barks at the crowd. He stands slightly shorter than most men, but overcomes his lack of altitude by finding anything, including other people, to stand on and tower above the crowds. He often hawks the shows while walking on tall stilts, wearing a blood red vest with long coat tails encrusted with glittering dark gems, dark blue pants as long as the stilts, and a small top hat on his head, the same style costume he wears in the Big Top when introducing the acts. He does so gleefully, with a booming voice that fills you with excitement, wonder, and slight trepidation as to what the circus holds. Stretched across his tanned face is a smile both broad and genuine, but his eyes sparkle with mischief. Cameron claims to have elfling blood in his ancestry, saying that is where he gets his mischievous and handsome qualities from.

Background

Cameron was born the runt of the large family that has run the circus for four generations. Through bravado, vigor, and near dwarven levels of tenacity, he has surpassed his older, more naturally talented family to take over as Ringmaster and run the circus. During his reign, he has reinvented the organization several times, bringing more success than the circus has seen in decades. Despite this, his troupe hasn't yet made it into the top rank of the touring spectacles. Among his fellow travelers, some follow him fervently, while others despise him and try to sabotage his efforts. There are many rumors about his notorious liaisons with the ladies. He perpetuates these rumors to try and fill the void of heartache left by Margo, the contortionist, who does not return his love.

Motivations

Cameron has only recently — roughly four years past — taken over the circus as ringmaster and is

Illustration by Michael Bielaczyc

still struggling to fill his uncle's shoes. He works daily to update the circus to compete with the renowned Royal Circus. He desperately wants his circus to be seen as the world's best, but struggles with his inner fears that it never will be. The workers will tell you that he is constantly pushing his "family" to try for bigger gigs, stunts, and spectacles, even if some will get hurt or lose their positions as the circus advances.

If you get on Margo's good side, Cameron will befriend you in hope of getting information on the hard-to-get lady. He can be bribed with gifts, which he prefers to be given to Margo on his behalf.

Cameron is worried about the sudden success of the circus and knows that it is not entirely from his hard work as ringmaster. He has noticed strange, glazed expressions on the guests, and some have begun to rally the locals against the circus. In his heart, he suspects sinister magic dwells beneath his big top; but thus far, he has failed to take into consideration any ominous implications, as that would deny his recent success.

Adventure Hooks

- Cameron is very protective of his "family." If he sees the adventurers pushing his performers too severely, he will intervene. He will not tolerate any abuse of his people.
- Cameron highly suspects that Rosaga and her daughters are helping the circus with mystical forces. He knows deep down that these are abusive and dark powers; but currently, it benefits his show and his people. Not until he feels that Rosaga — or the darkness she plays with — threatens the troupe will he put his full strength toward ending it.

Hang-outs

- In front of the big top on stilts.
- At the drinking tent after the final show.
- At his vardo, a round-roofed, enclosed wagon.

Rumors

- The circus is doing better than it ever has. Partially true — It is doing better than it used to, but it is far from its heyday.
- Margo is one of the main attractions to the show. Partially true — While she is very popular, no one thing has the biggest draw.
- Bechim thinks the circus is too small for him, and he should be part of a bigger show or a playwright for a rich patron. True.

Adventure Clues

- Cameron saw Resly here a week ago, but he did not see where he frequented.
- Resly has always been very interested in stories from the East and the people that Cameron's show may have crossed paths with in those desolate lands.

JIRRIM FARR
The Strongest Man Alive

Jirrim towers a full head above average men — a dark, curly-haired head, to be exact. His height, combined with his thick muscles, can cause a person to feel incredibly intimidated; but this is balanced by his soft blue eyes and childlike smile. He will try to be helpful to the extreme unless severely provoked. His gentle patience and kind smile make many assume the large brute is all muscle, but he has great wisdom, and can quote every line of any famous playwright.

Background

Jirrim was born into the nobility of Bordon; but as a second son, he held no public office or sway within his family. He had no drive to be part of the ruling class, dreaming instead of being an actor or a soldier. Once he was of age, Jirrim and his childhood best friend, Terris, joined the military in hopes of finding glory that was not tied to an inheritance.

During his tour in the Bordon army, Jirrim traveled deep into the Wastes of the East. While on patrol with Terris, he was attacked by what could only be described as a walking corpse. Terris was caught unaware and was badly hurt, though Jirrim dispatched the unnatural creature with his mace. He brought Terris back to be treated, but Terris himself became possessed and began to kill his comrades. Jirrim wrestled his friend to the ground and tore his head off with his bare hands. After the incident, he was personally distraught and viewed superstitiously by his command, so he left the service. This brought shame to his family, and he was disowned and left without an estate. No theater would give the struggling young man a chance for fear of reprisal from his powerful family.

Alone, destitute and still mourning his lost comrade, Jarrim stumbled upon the circus. He found employment as a roustabout, setting up tents, pounding stakes, and carrying equipment. After a pair of draft horses fell ill, and Jirrim single-handedly accomplished their workload, he was hired as the circus strongman. His easy-going character and ability to perform every breathtaking feat Cameron suggested led the Ringmaster to promote him to a star attraction; and eventually, he became Cameron's trusted friend. To this day, he sends a portion of every month's pay to the family of his fallen comrade.

Jirrim usually keeps to himself after the show ends, often retiring to his tent, tormented by the memories of the past. However, on moonless nights, when he thinks nobody will see him, he ventures outside the circus into the countryside and sits silently, staring up at the stars in silent supplication to his gods to pay respect to his fallen comrades.

Motivations

At his core, Jirrim wants to please those around him. If threatened, he is more likely to scream the circus's secret phrase for help, "Hey, rube!" than break his pacifist morals. However, if those he cares about are truly threatened, he becomes a force that few could stop. His hope is that the circus can grow and present high-spectacle dramatic plays. He can be easily bribed with new manuscripts of famous and infamous playwrights, flavorful drinks, or high-protein foods.

Adventure Hooks

- Jirrim senses the problems with the circus and is less trusting than Cameron.
- Jirrim has expressed an interest in getting rid of Rosaga and her seers, but Cameron has always rebuffed these pleas.
- Jirrim would welcome an outside force removing those he sees as problems in the group.
- Jirrim is extremely loyal to Cameron and believes that the show would only get better with the removal of the darker sides of the show.
- He also believes that Cameron and Margo would make a good match, and he aids his friend's desire in any way possible.

Hang-outs

- After hours — At his vardo.
- After hours — Along the outskirts of the circus, in meditation.
- At the side stage during his Feats of Strength show.
- Any time when the circus is open and he doesn't have a show going on, he can be found carrying heavy bales of hay to feed the animals.

Rumors

- Davin owes the circus more than he can ever pay back. False — he owes a lot, but not more than he can pay off over the next decade.
- Rosaga was kicked out of her last traveling group. True.

Adventure Clues

- *I disliked the look of Resly, who tossed coin around too much and asked questions about things a good man would not.*
- *I often saw Resly spending time with Rosaga and Drake when he visited the circus.*

- *Resly seemed infatuated with Margo and often bought her drinks after her show.*
- *One night a week or so back, I visited the Ferryport graveyard to the east of the circus and city to pray and pay respect to my fallen comrades; and I saw Olesya skulking about the gravestones. I didn't say anything to her. I just slipped away quietly.*

MARGO EELEN
Margo the Magnificent, Acrobat, Contortionist, Costumer

Margo's long chestnut-brown hair cascades over the sharp lines of her strong shoulders. She is deeply muscled, while still keeping her feminine curves. Her looks turn many heads, which means the same patrons also toss in many coins when she passes her hat at the end of a show. Her acrobatics are done on her hands as often as her feet. Across her body, she wears a wide variety of stylish outfits, often blending high fashion with the rebellious cuts you'd never find among the upper crust. If you meet her eye, she will look at you confidently with her wry smile, almost challenging you to make things more interesting. If you get the chance to speak with her, she is feisty, competitive, and as ready to crack a joke as she is to crack some skulls.

Background

Margo is the youngest daughter of the world-famous Aerial Eelens of the Royal Circus. For seven generations, her family has performed the most daring of aerial stunts. They achieved this through rigorous training, intense focus, and strict adherence to the path their predecessors laid forth. Margo hated it. She found the ceaseless rules to be stifling and couldn't help but break them the moment a back was turned. Or worse yet, she'd run off with the kids from town to chase trouble like a dog after a cart.

Her time with the town kids taught her many things. The orphans showed Margo all the back alleys. Using her aerial training, she could swing across the clotheslines almost as fast as the kids could run beneath her. In exchange, they showed her how they could stumble into a passing merchant and lift his purse with the greatest of ease. In every town the circus traveled to, she met more street kids, learned more skills, and got into more trouble. This all came to a stop when she was caught stealing the Governor's undergarments. It helped that she had stolen them the day before and was caught returning them, but it didn't help that she'd bedazzled them with the wedding ring and jewels of his mistress's enraged husband.

Her family was angry, but they quickly forgave Margo. They tried to provide her with more creative outlets. This was when she discovered her love for costuming. Her designs were as wild as her antics, and, though beautiful, were too bizarre for the traditional ideals of the Royal Circus. She decided then that it was time for her to leave. She tried selling her designs in several cities, but only received mixed success. After a year of this, she happened upon the small, struggling circus that Cameron had recently taken over. He welcomed her with open arms. To him, her outrageous designs were exactly what his circus needed to stand out against the much more polished Royal Circus. She pushed herself to master everything her family didn't — chiefly ground-based stunts. She mastered acrobatics, juggling, clowning, and contortionism. She loved her family for providing her with the foundation of training to quickly master these skills, but was also glad to be out from under their thumb and able to explore new jobs.

Motivations

She wants to have fun and be the best at whatever she does. If there is a party or a brawl, she will be there. However, if the fight gets out of hand, Jirrim will quickly pull her out. She appreciates the Ringmaster's attention and is fond of him, but is insistent that she does not want to be tied down. She can be bribed with fancy material, games, or a drinking contest…though, beware, she can chug a beer in seventy-three different positions.

Adventure Hooks

- After her last show, Margo will be found in the drinking tent. If the adventurers seek information, Margo will offer her knowledge in a wager of any sort: drinking contest, feats of strength and balance, or even riddles. She is not a sore loser and will offer up knowledge if she is bested.
- If the adventurers notice her intricate clothing, she will take them to her vardo. As she approaches, she inserts a key from around her neck into a lock and pulls a lever. The side of the vardo lifts up on a hinge forming an awning above her head. She then pulls back two large swinging walls, like giant-sized doors, revealing wondrous costumes lining the insides of the walls. The inner surface that is revealed contains display cases that fold down on hinged arms to display elaborate masks, costume jewelry, footwear, and

ladies' undergarments. Though her prices are a little high, if the adventurers purchase anything, she will freely share information over a couple of glasses of Tyrian wine.
- She is very close-lipped about Cameron and his ability to run the circus. She thinks he is doing what he thinks best, and his beliefs allow the performers a freedom not seen in other shows.

Hang-outs

- Drinking tent.
- Heading into town, as she is always looking for new fabrics for costumes.
- Beside her vardo with customers viewing her costume shop.

Rumors

- Jirrim dislikes some of the other performers that he views as too dark, or too mysterious, such as Rosaga and her spawn. True.
- Davin once had a game of dice that scored him a night with a queen. True-ish. He did win a night with a noble's wife, but there are other details known only to Davin.
- Grigore wants to sell the show and settle down in a bigger city like Bordon. False.

Adventure Clues

- Margo is often hounded by Resly. Not only is he attracted to her, but he often interrogates her about her family's circus. He asks of her travels when she was young and of her time in the North and East. He becomes fascinated by any hint about magic, and he keeps a high tab at the bar in order to learn more.
- Lord Resly openly talks about his relationship with one of Rosaga's daughters, though he has never mentioned which one. He speaks often of his wife in soft tones, sounding almost respectful; but his advances betray his fidelity, showing his words are little more than some strange loyalty.
- Drake, who had his own crush on Margo, has often warned her against getting any closer to Resly, despite his coin and charisma.
- After the adventurers talk to Zenia: At a town to the North, a farmer disappeared the day before the Circus left. He was a loyal patron of Rosaga's, and Margo saw him enter her tent the night of the disappearance. When Margo confronted Rosaga, she denied it; and Davin corroborated her story.

GRIGORE TODAREN
Circus owner, Bechim's father,
Cameron's and Davin's uncle

Grigore is short and taut, his wiry muscles evident even under the silks he prefers to wear. The road has aged him, both physically and mentally. Deep wrinkles mar his chiseled face, and the makeup that once made him a dandy now only accentuates his age. Despite his weathered appearance, Grigore is only in his late forties. Bright green eyes still sparkle from under his dyed black eyebrows, and he still carries himself as a former ringmaster should.

Background

Grigore inherited the circus when his brother, Cameron's and Davin's father, passed — this when he was "already getting on in the years," as he says. While he enjoyed the attention it garnered him, he despised the responsibility. He raised Cameron and his siblings as his own, though he was a playboy and heavy drinker and often fell short, even in his own eyes. He enjoyed watching Cameron and his own son, Bechim, grow up together, where one had the ability to write the word, the other had the ability to perform. Cameron's natural ability to connect with people, even with his lack of finesse, led Grigore to name him as the Ringmaster. His son still has not forgiven him for this choice, but Grigore knows it to be the correct one. A frontman must be larger than life, shining brighter than the other stars and making others aspire to be in his place. But to be a good leader, one cannot shine too brightly, and the spotlight must be shared.

Motivations

Grigore doesn't care much for running the show. At this point in his life, he wants the easy income his position allows and to spend his days flirting with the patrons while telling jokes at the drinking tent.

Adventure Hooks

- Grigore doesn't want anything to hurt the circus and will do whatever it takes to insure its safety.
- Grigore can be found in the drinking tent or out wandering amongst the crowd at the circus. He loves telling stories and will engage in small talk out and about, but will really share some yarns over a drink or two. (If the SG has the *Elves of Uteria* or *The Wanderer's Guide to Ferryport*, this is a great opportunity to insert relevant history of the region into the campaign.)

Hang-outs

- Drinking tent.
- Gambling tent.
- Wandering in the crowds telling stories of old.

Rumors

- Margo is asexual and completely uninterested in either sex. False.
- Zenia, the bearded princess, and Jirrim have had a romantic fling for some time. False — Despite her feelings, Jirrim has never been anything more than a friend for her.

Adventure Clues

- *I do recall seeing Lord Resly having a heated argument with one of Rosaga's daughters a couple of weeks back, but I don't know which one. They often dress alike, and it was dark.*
- *Rosaga is our fortune teller. She and her daughters came from another show. I don't know which show it was, or where it traveled; but she said she lost her husband due to some sort of accident there and could not stand the thought of working there any longer.*

BECHIM TODAREN
Playwright and son of Grigore

A tall man, muscular in his earlier years, but turning a little softer as he adds cycles past his 30th. He spends most of his time in his vardo writing, but can be seen running from show to show, making sure that everything is running smoothly. He dresses in immaculately-cleaned silks, doing his best to emulate the styles of the eastern region of Tyr. His tanned face breaks into the same smile as his cousin Cameron, though his brow is deeply creased over worrying eyes.

Background

The only son of Grigore Todaren and the only one of that line who stayed within the circus trade, Bechim assumed he would inherit the circus. When Cameron was given the Ringmaster's bullhorn, he was disappointed, but instead delved deep into his writing. If he was not to become famous through the leadership of the circus, he would write plays that would be performed from Ish to the Wastes.

Motivations

Bechim is happy to have time to himself, although he would love to run the circus. He looks to expand the reach and fame of his writing and will bargain with anyone who can offer him some notoriety.

Adventure Hooks

- Bechim seems to be everywhere in the circus during work hours, making sure things run smoothly. Afterwards, he is usually in his trailer, unless there is someone important to meet with. If he feels someone can advance his fame as a writer, he will freely give any information he has about the circus.
- Even though he enjoys his time alone, he also enjoys the company of attractive companions. He is interested in both genders, as long as they are intelligent and attractive. With a little Tyrian wine, he opens up about many things.

Hang-outs

- His vardo.
- Drinking tent.
- At the front gate.
- Backstage at some of the more theatrical shows.

Rumors

- Zenia has said she will shave her famous beard and settle down if only the right man would ask for her hand. True — If that man is Jirrim.
- Cameron knows who Resly is, but he claims that he hasn't had any direct dealings with him. False.

Adventure Clues

- Rosaga has many after-hours visitors in each city or town that they stop in.
- Resly once offered him patronage to become an in-house writer for him — not for plays or prose, but instead to write legal documents and governmental papers.

DAVIN TODAREN

Black sheep, Gambler, Reader, brother to Cameron

Unlike his younger brother Cameron, Davin is tall, with broad shoulders and delicate, clever hands. He taps out a complex rhythm on the table, drawing you in closer. The man's eyes are a blue so pale they're the color of polished steel. They look strange against his tan skin and dark hair.

He lounges on a barrel and seems to be in a state of ease. A closer look shows you that his light eyes restlessly dart back and forth. When his gaze falls upon you, it's almost tangible…as if, with a glance, he browses through your belongings, learning your weight, age, history, and value. It sends goosebumps down your arms.

Background

Life always came easily to Davin. He's the tallest and strongest of the Todaren children. When they would play games, he would win, whether because of his natural athleticism or his willingness to bend the rules. When it came to learning the circus arts, he was a natural. What others took months to learn, he could do in hours. Because of this, he grew bored easily, rarely practiced beyond basic mastery and often made fun of those who didn't learn as quickly. Chief among those was his brother Cameron. He never understood why Cameron would work so hard to learn skills others could be easily manipulated to do.

The one thing that did hold his attention was gambling. He loved the high stakes, fickleness of luck, and challenge of outsmarting the system. Like all things, he excelled at it. Only the softest silks graced his limbs, the finest wines sated his thirst, and the highest stakes satisfied his boredom.

His life took a sharp turn when a bet went bad and, as a result, the Todaren's almost lost their circus. He claims he was cheated, but the family still cut him off from their funds. Soon after, his studious show-off of a brother, Cameron, was advanced to Ringmaster. He now spends his time as one of Rosaga's readers, his good looks and charm bringing many court ladies — and their purses — into the fortune-teller's tent.

Motivations

He uses his skills at reading and manipulating others to convince them he's reading their minds or bringing forth the spirit of a loved one to communicate with. Lately his ability to do this has become unnaturally accurate, thanks to training from Rosaga.

He is furious to be passed over as Ringmaster and knows it's only a matter of time before Cameron will screw up and they'll all beg him to take over. He wants to use the circus's money to pay off his debts and then reward those who are loyal to him.

Adventure Hooks

- Davin loves gambling and games of chance. He will offer information if the pot looks deep enough.
- He will fall for some bribes, but he is good at reading people and will offer bad information if he thinks they are gullible enough.

Hang-outs

- Fortuneteller's tent.
- Gambling tent.

Rumors

- Cameron has taken quite a few donations from the Resly estate, which has made Ferryport one of the most successful stops for the show. True.
- If the players seem particularly astute, Davin will tell the truth and offer: *"Jirrim often goes out on nights when no moon is in the sky and pays respect to his fallen friends."* However, if they seem gullible, he may choose to lie and mislead them, stating: *"While, outwardly, Jirrim dislikes violence, some suspect him of leaving the show on dark nights to enact revenge against patrons who have disrespected the 'family'."*

Adventure Clues

- Davin knows what Rosaga can really do, but he would only give her up to a king's ransom worth of bribing. Note: if the players prevent the escaped circus beast from wreaking havoc, Davin may be in their debt, since he is the one who left its pen unlatched.
- He knows that Resly's wife was killed, but does not know who did it. He overheard Rosaga and Olesya whispering about her.

ZENIA, THE BEARDED MISTRESS OF THE BEASTS

Beast Tamer

The woman is a delicate flower. She stands barely above five feet tall, with a curved figure and petite waist. She is from Tyr and has the Eastern features of olive brown skin and long, dark black hair. Much like the flowers that she wears in her braids, her hair flows like a ring of petals around her head. From scalp to chin, it is thick and luxurious. It is her beard hair that most catches the eye. It's soft as silk, and somehow doesn't make her look manly — probably because she carries herself with grace and approaches everyone with motherly kindness.

Background

Little is known about where she came from, though those closest to her know she was sold into slavery at a young age. When she hit puberty, her beard began to come in; and the circus gladly purchased her. Barra Todaren, Cameron's deceased mother, was impressed by Zenia's inner fire, courage, and work ethic. She immediately freed Zenia and offered her a place in their family.

For eight years she has toured with the circus, glad to be set free, but ever feeling the outcast because of the beard. She's learned to live with the insults, stares, and questions. Despite this, there is a sadness in her

beautiful eyes that has slightly diminished since Jirrim joined the family. She was immediately drawn to his gentle strength and finds his troubled past something she can relate to. He is her best friend.

Motivations

She knows the beard is the reason for her freedom and income. Despite this, she secretly resents it and wishes a man could see past it to the woman underneath. She is hopeful Jirrim will be that man. She is very smart and intuitive. Many of the circus come to her for advice. If approached gently, she will give knowledge and advice to help the adventurers. If she is pressed hard, Jirrim will come to her aid.

Adventure Hooks

- Zenia is fascinated by the thought of knowing the future and is close friends with Anva, who uses Zenia's naivety to make herself look better. She feeds Zenia false visions of a happy life with Jirrim's children. Zenia will stand up for Anva and her family with every breath.
- Zenia can often be seen with Jirrim or watching his shows when she is not performing her own.

Hang-outs

- Animal pens.
- With Jirrim.

Rumors

- Jirrim dislikes all things related to the Never*, and he actively researches subjects relating to magic. True.
- Margo is very observant; nothing seems to miss her; and she often brings up the mishaps she sees in jest after a few drinks. True.
- Grigore was in love with Cameron's mother, though his brother won her heart. True.

Adventure Clues

- Zenia may mislead the adventurers through her own lack of knowledge of what the Babicova family plans.
- Though Zenia likes and trusts Anva, she found a note a couple weeks back dropped from Anva's pouches in Zenia's tent. It was from Lord Resly to Anva and was intimate and uncomfortable for her to read. She burned the note later that night; but it made her wonder, if Anva would hide this from her, what else was she dishonest about?

* *The Never is the common name for the Navirim, which many believe is a parallel world — a dream-like world inhabited by the things that haunt our own nightmares.*

DRAKE THE DRAGONMAN

Drake is tall and thin, but well-muscled. He gets his name from a skin condition that causes most of his body to be covered in a knobby texture resembling scales. He has also tattooed most of his body to accentuate his draconian looks and walks about clad in only a short kilt most of the time to show off his tattoos and muscles. His bald head sports exotic tattoos that make him resemble the dragons of myth.

Background

Born in the Eastern Wastelands, he was abandoned as a baby and found by a hermit who lived in the Wastes by herself. She raised him and taught him the ways of the wild, as well as honing his ability with the Arts. He showed a particular talent for summoning and controlling fire. She told him to forever keep their secret, that none may know that he has the wild magical abilities that came naturally to him. She foresaw that he would be bullied and shunned because of his appearance and decided to call him 'Drake' meaning 'Dragon' in the old tongue, to embrace his difference and make him sound tough. When she passed of old age, he found the circus and joined. His appearance, coupled with his ability to summon fire, made him a crowd favorite.

His show combines feats of strength as well as things like lifting heavy stones with his earrings, or hammering a nail into his nostril. He always ends his performance with a fire show, where he seems to unnaturally spew flames from his mouth or toss balls of fire which dance among the audience. His best shows are when Cameron joins him and they improv together, juggling and playing among the flames.

Motivations

Drake enjoys his place at the show. He provides muscle when needed; but besides that, he performs his shows and interacts with the patrons. He has a crush on Margo, and sometimes lets this get the better of his judgement when discussing the other performers. He knows something is rotten within the circus and hopes to root out the darkness and expel it from the show that he loves so much.

Adventure Hooks

- Drake breaks up a brawl in the drinking tent and ends up using a small bit of wild magic that the adventurers would notice.

- Drake is protective of the show and will approach the adventurers to see what they are so interested in, and what they have learned.

Hang-outs

- Walking the lanes.
- Outside of his stage talking to patrons.

Rumors

- Cameron is a good man, but he is unsuited for Margo. Too many patrons like him, and it's better for a Ringmaster to be uninhibited in a love life. Opinion.
- Anva, the fortune teller Rosaga's oldest daughter, is strange. She is always interested in what Drake is doing, but she is evasive about her own life. True — her interest is in his wild magic, but he does not know that.
- Resly was always trying to have his way with the performers, and Drake often cautioned him about his ways. On a couple of occasions, he was in heated arguments with the nobleman. True.

Adventure Clues

- *I fear there is something evil and unnatural about the circus of late.*
- *In the past year or so, the show has fallen into some trouble in various towns and cities. There have been accusations of foul play as locals have disappeared when the show is in town.*
- *The magistrates never found any of the missing people or evidence of any wrongdoing at the circus, but we moved on quickly.*
- *Now that Lord and Lady Resly are missing as well, I fear it is starting all over again.*

ROSAGA BABICOVA
The Fortune Teller

Rosaga is the circus's fortune teller, but is secretly a member of the Sworn[5]. It is hard to pinpoint her age, as her bright red hair and blue eyes seem timeless. Her clothes emphasize the stereotype of the gypsy, and her jewelry and makeup add mystique.

Background

Rosaga was not always with the Todaren Family Circus. She was previously a palm reader at a smaller show in the far North. She was married and had children. Money was good, jobs were plenty, and her family had little want for anything. But this seemingly mundane story has a much darker side.

---

[5] THE SWORN — The Sworn are a society that stretches across the known lands of Uteria, who look to improve culture and society in the world. They are detailed more in the previous adventure module, *The Goblins of Kaelnor Forest* (FA01).

Her husband, Conall, was the Two-Faced Man, a conjoined twin. He was the dominant twin, able to speak, walk and be a part of the world around him. His brother, Kier, who existed only as a malformed face on the right side of his brother's head with a small almost-useless arm, was not so lucky. His only way to communicate was through notes scrawled by his small, handicapped hand. As the relationship between Rosaga and Conall progressed over the years, she realized that the mind of Kier was much more like hers — sharp, intelligent, and hungry. She had then only begun to dabble in the real magic arts, and she shared the few old tomes she had with Kier. Conall cared nothing for the books or magic, his only concern being for the show and the patrons.

During this time, the circus hit hard times; and Conall began to drink, growing abusive toward his family. Rosaga found that she was falling in love with Kier rather than his drunkard brother, and Kier resented his imprisonment within his brother's body. So they worked out a plan to separate Kier from his twin, exchanging notes whenever Conall passed out from drink.

It was then that, in their dreams, there came a spirit who claimed to be Kaldrath, who some in Uteria worship as a god. It is believed that he has long been imprisoned between the worlds of Uteria and the Navirim. He guided the two fledgling mages in learning a dark ritual to finally free Kier from his brother. It would kill the body they both shared but Kier's consciousness would be pulled into the Navirim, where he could survive until Rosaga gained the skills to bring him back to life in a new body in Uteria. The ritual worked, though many of her old circus mates accused her of killing her husband, and she and her children were chased from the show. She told her children that the old Ringmaster killed their father, but she knew a way to bring him back, though it might take many years.

Since that night, she has served Kaldrath, progressing in power and knowledge, seeking to bring her love back into her world.

Motivations

Rosaga is close to achieving her goal. She trained Lord Resly and used his wife's body as an experiment to bring over a consciousness from the Navirim. This dark fey would then help her bring Kier back from the Navirim. She will turn the adventurers around as much as she can, hoping that nothing stops her from completing her ritual. She is just waiting for the Sirin she brought into Lady Resly's body to gain back enough strength to aid in the ritual. She plans on

Illustration by A.L. Ashbaugh

killing Davin and using his body for Kier.

Rosaga has been using her abilities to placate and make the minds of the circus patrons more malleable. Once a day, they have a "show" featuring acts of fortune telling, fireworks, and mytacism. As her young daughters entrance the crowd with their

23

showmanship and good looks, Rosaga charms them with an ancient ritual and artifact that was passed down to her from her grandmother, who received it from her grandmother before her, along with the ritual to activate it. It allows her to expand her charm spells over the whole crowd in her tent. The patrons leave a little glassy-eyed and more willing to spend a little at the circus. As of late, Rosaga has also experimented with taking a little of the crowd's life force and weaving that into the magic show they are attending, creating bigger fireworks or even summoning creatures "from another world" to answer questions for those who attend.

The Lyre of Taldos

Rosaga's family has passed down an ancient musical artifact, known as the Lyre of Taldos, from generation to generation, teaching their daughters by word of mouth only the ritual of how to use the artifact. Making it function requires the player to master playing a complex song on the lyre while performing a slow dance. Rosaga has not yet taught her daughters the ritual; so if she is killed, the ritual will be lost with her. The lyre doesn't look like it would be worth anything. It's a very old lyre; the hollow body is made from what appears to be a tortoise shell, while the hollow yokes are made from the horns of a wyvere. The strings are made from the intestines of a long-forgotten beast.

Malynn has heard of Rosaga's shows and suspects she is using a spell or magic item to boost the effect of her spells. He wants to retrieve the item for study by the Tower. If the PCs somehow manage to find and take the lyre from Rosaga's tent, he will bargain with them for it, pointing out that the item is useless to them, since they do not know the ritual to activate it.

Powers/Functions: The Lyre gives its user the ability to extend and empower mind-influencing spells. It also gives the user a +10 to intimidate and diplomacy checks.

Adventure Hooks

- Rosaga will avoid the adventurers as much as she can. If she has to speak to them, she will admit to being close to Resly, but only for his money. She will say he is a lush and an adulterer.
- She will say that Margo used to spend way too much time with him, and she doesn't have to read fortunes to see that they had a complicated relationship.

Hang-outs
- Her tent.

Rumors
- Cameron has taken quite a few donations from the Resly estate, which has made Ferryport one of the most successful stops for the show. True.

Adventure Clues
- Rosaga will not give any clues, and if anything, she will use her charm to turn the adventurers in another direction.

ANVA
Rosaga's daughter, Fortune Teller

Anva is Rosaga's older daughter at 22 cycles and remembers her father, unlike Oleysa. Anva remembers her father's drunken rages and the sad eyes of her uncle. She also has real magical powers, unlike her younger sister. Anva has had a fling with Lord Resly for years, each time the circus comes to town. Her mother has encouraged that relationship in order to gain Resly's trust, so as to take advantage of his great influence.

Anva specializes in performing readings for people, using Tarot cards.

Rumors

- In a drunken fit of rage, Bechim once killed a male companion who questioned his ability to write. False — Bechim once beat a man close to death, but did not kill him.
- Cameron uses his "unnatural" charm to keep his people in line. Some believe it borders on the supernatural. False: he has no special abilities beyond his natural charm and other talents.

Adventure Clues

- Anva will speak to the players the moment they enter the tent. She knew they would be coming. She will lie and say that a wandering warlock came and tried to bother her family. He was bearded and "went by the name Malin or such." He was seen arguing with Resly a few days ago, then following him as he left the circus.
- She will push the adventurers to look closer at Bechim.

OLESYA
Rosaga's daughter, Palm Reader

Olesya dislikes her mother and older sister, but is afraid to leave because she is only thirteen. She will actively try to out them and their plots; but sadly, she knows very little of what her mother and sister really do.

Encounter

Olesya specializes in reading people's palms. If the adventurers visit her mother's tent, she will approach them shortly after they leave. If the players don't eventually visit her mother's tent, the SG should have her approach them in the crowd or wherever they are at an appropriate time and attempt to converse with them under the guise of reading their palms. She has seen them going about asking questions, and word travels fast in the circus. She wants to find out if they might be able to help her, but she is very nervous.

Rumors

- Her mother Rosaga was in love with her husband's brother. True.
- Her mother told her and her sister that their father Conall was killed by the ringmaster of the circus they used to travel with. (It is true that Rosaga told her girls this, but it was Rosage who caused his death.)
- Grigore believes Bechim is too self-centered to run the circus. That is why he chose Cameron. Bechim is aware of his father's opinion of him. True.

Adventure Clues

- *Resly comes to our tent often each year when we visit Ferryport.*
- *Lately, I have seen Resly bringing packages to my mother and leaving with other packages, but I don't know what was in them.*
- *One night, I gathered my courage and followed him as he left. He entered a large Ferryport graveyard to the east of the circus. I was fearful, but I followed him in. He had disappeared. I had a bad feeling that I should get out of there, and fled back to the circus.*

OTHER BACKGROUND CHARACTERS

These characters do not play a part of the main story, but can be used as background flavor of the circus.

1. **Jans the Gamemaster** — He grew up in the high society of Jaeldor, but left because he hated the politics. He loves designing games for the circus and will actively gamble with any who wish to try their hand at winning his games.
2. **Kaia the Sword Swallower** — She grew up poor, but her charm and ability to swallow most anything has put money in her pocket. She does

not care for the happenings around the show as long as she gets her coin.

3. **Deen, the Priest of Rindelbok** — Deen runs the gambling tent and has a sleight of hand show in the same tent each night. He enjoys slightly teasing the patrons and thinks that everyone in the "mundane world could use a little shake up."

SHOWS!

Each performer at the Circus has their own show, as well as some shared shows. Some shows are free and the performer passes their hat for a tip at the end; but the big shows are a copper apiece, collected at the entrance of the big top tent.

Big Shows

- **Barely Balanced Acrobatics and Fire Show!** — Cameron, Margo, and Jirrim perform in this big top show. It is a sight to behold as they perform juggling, contortions, and fire, all in the finale show. At the end, small fireworks erupt within the tent.
- **Drake's Firewhip Show** — Drake performs with dual flaming whips while other jugglers work the outer ring with their own fire poi and hoops.
- **Rosaga and Families Supernatural Show of the Arts** — In Rosaga's tent, she and her daughters perform feats of illusion for those who will pay a copper to enter.

Other Shows

- **The Exotic Creature Show** — Xenia parades her animals in the animal pen and has the trained animals perform tricks.
- **Jirrim, the Strongest Man in the West** — Jirrim's solo show, performed in the smaller stage, where he exhibits feats of strength and wonder.

OPTIONAL ENCOUNTERS AT THE CIRCUS

ENCOUNTER — *The Drunken Brawl*

Hafsha, an out-of-work mercenary from the southlands, is drunk and looking for attention in the drinking tent. When the waitresses spurn his advances, and Margo turns him down, he gets violent.

The brawl will start in the back corner around Hafsha. Margo just brushed off his overly aggressive advances and Jirrim has moved in to calm to situation. Caught off guard, Hafsha breaks his ceramic tankard on the side of Jirrim's face. Others sitting at the table with Hafsha jump up and begin to shout. A bouncer comes in to break it up and Hafsha grabs him and throws him into Jirrim and the crowd. Others, excited by the show and wits dulled by alcohol, join in. A barroom fight in a traveler's tent is much less likely to draw the attention or long term problems with the city guards…

Brawl Events

- A farmer throws a chair at one of the adventurers. Reflex save, DC 15 or take 1d3 subdual damage.
- A keg gets turned over, making a 15' section of the floor extremely slippery. To fight on the slippery floor, it takes a DC 15 Acrobatics check.
- A support pole gets pulled down, and part of the tent collapses.
- Someone shouts for muscle from the circus. 2 rounds later four men, including Drake, run in and help calm down the crowd.

Brawl Conclusions

- If the players use non-subdual damage, they will be reported to the city guards and may face jail time. Though a well-placed bribe may keep them out.
- Should the adventurers end up helping Jirrim and Margo, they will receive a +5 to their diplomacy with them and will have a higher chance of learning all the clues the two know. To help, all they need to do is help subdue Hafsha and his thugs.

HAFSHA   CR 2

Hafsha is tall and well-muscled, though he is starting to show his 46 cycles. He has dark brown skin and very short black and gray hair. He is not looking to kill anyone, just hurt them. He will use anything nearby as a bludgeoning weapon, most likely a table leg.

XP 600
Male Middle-aged Human Fighter 3
None Medium humanoid (human)
Init −2
Senses Perception +0

DEFENSE

AC 14, touch 8, flat-footed 14 (+6 armor, −2 Dex)
hp 25 (3d10+7)
Fort +4, Ref −1, Will +1, +1 Will vs. Fear

OFFENSE

Speed 30 ft.

STATISTICS

STR 17, DEX 6, CON 13, INT 9, WIS 11, CHA 10
Base Atk +3; **CMB** +6; **CMD** 14 (15 vs. disarm) (15 vs. grapple)
Feats Catch Off-Guard, Cleave, Power Attack, Quick Draw, Toughness
Skills Acrobatics +0 , Climb +7 , Handle Animal +4, Intimidate +6
Languages Common
Special Qualities Armor Training, Bonus CMD, Bonus Feat, Bonus Feats, Bravery, Skilled

---

STREET THUGS (3)   CR 1

Hafsha's companions

XP 400 each
Human Fighter 1/Rogue 1
NE Medium humanoid
Init +2
Senses Perception +5

DEFENSE

AC 15, touch 12, flat-footed 13 (+3 armor, +2 Dex)
hp 16 (2 HD; 1d10+1d8+6)
Fort +3, Ref +4, Will +0

OFFENSE

Speed 30 ft.
Melee Quarterstaff +4 (1d6+3) or Quarterstaff +2/+2 (1d6+3/1d6+1) or Dagger +4 (1d4+3/19–20) or Sap +4 (1d6+3 nonlethal)
Ranged Dagger +3 (1d4+3/19–20)
Special Attacks Sneak Attack +1d6

STATISTICS

STR 16, DEX 15, CON 13, INT 8, WIS 10, CHA 12
Base Atk +1; **CMB** +4; **CMD** 16
Feats Skill Focus (Intimidate), Toughness, Two-Weapon Fighting
Skills Climb +8, Intimidate +9, Knowledge (local) +4, Perception +5 (+6 to find traps), Stealth +7
Languages Common
Special Qualities Trapfinding +1
Gear Masterwork Studded Leather, Daggers (2), Quarterstaff, Sap, Manacles (2)
Boon A street thug could attempt to kidnap or threaten a particular NPC, deliver a message, or create a disturbance with a street brawl whose distraction causes a −2 penalty on opposed Perception checks for 1 minute.

Illustration by Christopher Burdett

ENCOUNTER — *The Loose Thundrom*
(XP 700 – 1500)

As the players are making their way through the circus, they hear screams. Read the following:

Patrons of the show have started shouting and running back and forth in the muddy lanes. A yak-like creature larger than a draft horse, its long shaggy fur now coated in mud, is barreling down the space between tents straight toward you! A large, brightly colored yoke hangs from its long tusks, and gleaming gold decorations adorn large, curled, ram-like horns.

This Thundrom is part of Zenia's beast tamer show and is somewhat tame. Davin, who is in charge of feeding the animals in the show due to his debt to the circus, accidentally left the gate unlocked after the last feeding. Some local troublemakers sneaked in and spooked the creature, which led it to burst free and stampede down the roadways. It is a newly added creature to the show, and while normally well controlled by Zenia, being free among so many people has completely spooked it.

THUNDROM   CR 2
XP 700
N Large beast
Init +2
Senses Low Light Vision, Scent, Perception +8

DEFENSE
AC 17, touch 12, flat footed 13 (+3 dex, +4 natural armor, −1 size)
hp 23 (2d8+10)
Fort +8, Ref +7, Will +3

OFFENSE
Speed 50 ft.
Melee Bite +5 (1d6 + 3), Slam +1 (1d8 + 2)
Space 10 ft.
Reach 5 ft.

STATISTICS
STR 20, **DEX** 16, **CON** 21, **INT** 2, **WIS** 17, **CHA** 9
Base Atk +1; **CMB** +7; **CMD** 21
Feats Endurance, Run
Skills Survival +2, Perception +8

ECOLOGY
Environment Mountain
Organization Solitary, pair, herd
Treasure n/a

Thundrom are large hairy beasts from the Swordspyne Mountains. They are used as mounts by the people of the mountains; but to most of those in the plains, the Thundrom seems exotic and strange.

Thundroms are a little larger and bulkier than a horse and are covered in shaggy brown hair. Their bodies resemble that of a yak in shape, but they have long tusks and even longer curled ram-like horns. Its head looks large for its body, its four nostrils the only exposed skin on this otherwise long haired beast.

If the players decide to help, there are multiple ways to try and pacify the creature. If an adventurer has Wild Empathy, the DC to calm the creature is DC 18. The players can also attack it, using subdual or full damage, though either way the Thundrom will attack back in full if anything tries to hurt it in its current mental state.

To add onto of the mess, two locals will run up with clubs and try to "aid" in subduing the animal. If the adventurers try and stop them from harming the Thundrom, they will turn on them (having had a little too much to drink at the drinking tent).

During the encounter, after 2 rounds, Davin will arrive and shout to the group not to harm the creature. He will do what he can to help and try to keep the crowd back. He is useless with the frightened animal, but can make the drunk patrons back down if the PCs have not already. If the adventurers are able to subdue, induce sleep, or otherwise calm the creature, Davin will be very grateful, as he would have been in a lot of trouble if either the animal or any patrons were injured or killed, which could mean the Ferryport official would ask them to leave.

After four rounds, Zenia will run up and shout, "Don't hurt her, she's just scared!", and will do her best to help calm it as well, if the PCs have not already handled the situation. (She has Wild Empathy with a bonus of +4).

If the players kill the poor frightened beast, they gain 700 XP for defeating it, but will earn the enmity of Zenia. She will go to find Camron to try to get him to kick them out. If they subdue the animal without significantly harming it, they instead gain 1000 XP. If they prevent any bystanders from coming to harm in the process, they gain an additional 250 XP. Finally, if they manage to keep the drunk locals from harming the beast, they gain an additional 250 XP, for a total possible 1500 XP.

If the Thundrom is subdued without harm, Zenia will open up to the characters with many more clues, and even give them two applications of a Tyrian salve which will help any wounds they may have incurred. Even if they were not harmed, the SG may choose to have her offer them some salve as a reward, especially if they do not have a powerful healer, as they will probably need healing before the night is over.

Tyrian Healing Salve: Heals 1d6 damage. Takes 2 rounds to apply. DC 25 Alchemy check to create, +2 if you have profession herbalist. Worth 40 gp per dose.

ENCOUNTER — *The Pickpocket (XP 200)*
As the players walk around the circus, they become a target for Fitz, a young street thief. Fitz will attempt to pickpocket them, and may go completely unnoticed. Fitz will not try and fight the adventurers if he is caught, instead trying his best to escape and run, using his caltrops and dexterity to his best advantage.

Pickpocket Attempt
Fitz will target the character who looks to have the most coin and try to lift their coin purse. DC 20 Sleight of hand check, and Fitz has a +12 to it. The target rolls a Perception check vs the Sleight of Hand check.

If Fitz is caught, he will try to bargain for his freedom. He has been casing the circus for weeks, so he will know a couple of the rumors that the circus performers know (SG's pick). Earn 200 XP.

Adventure Clues
- *"Ther' was another man, short, didn't like the look of His Highness. He came 'round and was askin' questions, and got kicked out of the circus. Who comes into a circus with a patrol of guards at your back?"*
- *"That old fortune teller, I don't like the look of her. She gots something though, something she keeps under her robes during her show, but she touches it a lot. Don't know, she creeps me out, and I felt funny after I saw that damn show."*

FITZ
CR 1/2

Fitz is young, though his skin is crisscrossed with small scars, showing his rough upbringing. Black hair hangs limply around his face and often covering his eyes. His clothing is worn, but non-descript, with enough layers to keep him warm on winter nights.

XP 200
Human Rogue 1
N Medium humanoid
Init +3
Senses Perception +3

DEFENSE
AC 14, touch 12, flat-footed 12 (+1 armor, +3 Dex)
hp 6 (1d8+1)
Fort +1, Ref +5, Will −1

OFFENSE
Speed 30 ft.
Melee Sap +0 (1d6 nonlethal)
Ranged Dart +3 (1d4)
Special Attacks Sneak Attack +1d6

STATISTICS
STR 10, DEX 17, CON 12, INT 14, WIS 9, CHA 14
Base Atk +0; **CMB** +0; **CMD** 13
Feats Deft Hands, Skill Focus (Sleight of Hand)
Skills Acrobatics +7, Appraise +5, Bluff +6, Disable Device +9, Disguise +8, Escape Artist +7, Knowledge (local) +5, Perception +3 (+4 to find traps), Sense Motive +3, Sleight of Hand +12, Stealth +7
Languages Common, Halfling
Special Qualities Trapfinding +1
Combat Gear Bag of Caltrops
Other Gear Padded Armor, Darts (4), Sap, Disguise Kit, Thieves' Tools
Boon A pickpocket can attempt to steal a small item for the PCs or plant a small item on a target.

ENCOUNTER — *Malynn and Lorthain*
After the adventurers have spent some time around the circus, they are approached by two men. One is medium height and build, and the other is thickly muscled and bald. This encounter should only happen after the players have started to put together their own ideas about what is happening around the circus.

Malynn will only approach them if he feels he can get some information from them as well, or if one of the PCs has used magic openly in some way.

Read the following:

As you make your way around the festivities, the crowd seems to part and two men walk directly toward you. One is tall and bald; old iron and steel armor covers him from neck to toes and a large double-handed sword hangs at his back. The other is shorter and thinner of build, his fine clothes a little travel worn, but showing some strange adornments and symbols, hinting at distant lands and mysterious wards. He smiles, his trimmed dark goatee framing bright white teeth. "Well now, isn't this an interesting group? And seemingly as interested in this traveling show as we are. I am Malynn Andros, traveler from the Tower; and this is my friend Lorthain. Who might you all be?"

Malynn is interested in anything the adventurers say, truth or not. If any of them are magic users, he will seem to pay close attention to them. He will offer little in the way of knowledge about the show, but he will gladly tell them that he is here on order of the Tower. Rumors of misuse of magic in the area, as well as the closeness of the re-emerged forest elves has piqued the interest of the Tower. He will not detain them, but offers to meet them later in the evening in the drinking tent.

MALYNN ANDROS
Malynn is a man of medium height, but many feel he towers over them. His dark hair is speckled with a little gray, but he still looks no older than his late twenties. His piercing blue eyes and commanding personality fill any room he is in. Many in the city consider him dangerous, as he has made no secret of his ability with magic.

Background
Malynn is a member of the Otari[6]. The Tower sent him to keep eyes on the events within the city. Malynn is especially interested in the interactions between this new government and the newly integrated "non-humans." Malynn has passed off his visit to the city as a representative of the city of Tyr. With Tyr so far to the East, no one has reason to question him.

Motivations
Malynn is in the city for the Tower[7] only. He dislikes being away from the Tower and finds the

---

6   Otari is the formal name for the Mages of the Tower. More can be found out in *The Tome of the Arts* book.
7   For more information on the Tower, see the Magic supplement in this booklet located after the adventure.

lack of magic in the West disconcerting. His current concern is the circus and some of its performers. He suspects the seer and her family of ravaging, but he hopes to drive some bigger prey out into the open by giving them space. He is also interested in anyone he comes across with any talent in "The Art."

LORTHAIN TAMEN

Lorthain is a little taller than an average man, but his muscled frame makes him imposing. He is quiet and thoughtful, but when he is merry, his laugh fills the room. His hairless head makes him easy to pick out in a crowd, or find on a battlefield. His dark brown skin shows the scars and wrinkles of many decades of travel, looking to be over 40 cycles of age.

Background

Lorthain was born in the Tower; his father was a refugee from the Southern Empire of Ish. His father became an Archeon and his mother a librarian at the Tower. He enjoyed his time growing up among the ancient tomes and empty passages and took the mantle of Archeon with pride and reverence when he was old enough. He was assigned to Malynn when Malynn was a young initiate, as all Archeons are assigned to Luminar by the Tower; but they have grown to be good friends.

Motivations

Lorthain follows the law of the Tower to the letter. If someone is believed to be a Ravager, they must stand trial; and if found guilty, they are silenced. There is responsible use of magic and there is not, there is no gray to him in this area. His second goal is the protection of his friend Malynn.

If the adventurers end up in the drinking tent, Malynn will be waiting at a side table. He is playing a card and token game with his companion. When he sees the group, read the following.

Malynn smiles when he sees you enter the tent. His blue eyes sparkle as he motions to the empty seats next to him. His companion looks up for a moment, then back down to his cards. The table is littered with tokens of different colors and cards. He lays his cards down face up, and his companion grunts and tosses his cards down in a pile.

After looking about to make sure no one else appears to be listening, Malynn will ask the adventurers about themselves and their connection to the circus in hushed tones, looking for any new information since they last parted.

Adventure Clues — Malynn

Malynn will also offer some information about Rosaga, Cameron, and Lord Resly. His companion, Lorthain, will stay quiet during most of the conversation, but will answer questions if asked.

- *I think Cameron is a good man; but he knows something is wrong with some of his people, and he refuses to deal with it.*
- *Rosaga and her daughters seem suspicious; but so far we have not seen them do anything beyond parlor tricks. However, I caution you — if she is a Ravager, she may be more than you can handle alone.*
- *I believe there is more to Resly than meets the eye, and he is a person of interest to the Tower. However, I have not seen any solid evidence of wrongdoing on his part yet, other than reports of him skulking about the circus during and after hours.*

Adventure Clues — Lorthain

- *I sense there is something dark at the circus, and it needs to be stopped.*
- *We have only been in the city for a week and are still getting the lay of the land.*

If the group tells Malynn they are going to the graveyard, he will agree that is a good idea and states that he and Lorthain will continue searching for clues at the circus.

Malynn will also offer to share knowledge with any adventurer who uses magic. He will use this as a way to judge the intention of the wild mage. If he feels they may be a Ravager, he will capture the offending mage and try to "silence" them. This is also a way for a non-ravaging magic user to start on the path of luminar.

MALYNN   CR 5

Male Human Adept Luminar 6
Size: M
Space: 5 ft. x 5 ft.
Type Humanoid (Human)
HD (6d6); hp 24
Init +1 (+1 Dex, +0 Misc)
Vision AL: None

DEFENSE
AC 11 (touch 11, flatfooted 10)
Fort +2, Ref +3, Will +7

OFFENSE
Speed Walk 30 ft.

STATISTICS

STR 9, DEX 13, CON 10, INT 18, WIS 14, CHA 13

*Dagger +2 0 ft./PS (1d4–1 19–20/x2 Primary M) or *Dagger (Thrown) +4 10 ft./PS (1d4 19–20/x2 Primary M)

Feats Alertness, Combat Casting, Coordinated Maneuvers, Empower Spell, Persuasive

Skills Appraise +9, Craft (Alchemy) +9, Diplomacy +3, Heal +4, Intimidate +3, Knowledge (Arcana) +13, Knowledge (Dungeoneering) +10, Knowledge (Geography) +9, Knowledge (History) +13, Knowledge (Planes) +10, Knowledge (Religion) +8, Perception +9, Sense Motive +4, Sleight of Hand +3, Spellcraft +13, Survival +4

Special Qualities Arcane Bond (Su), Bonus Feat, Bonus Feats, Cantrips, Hand of the Apprentice (Su), Skilled, Universal School

Possessions 1 Dagger, 1 Traveler's Outfit, 1 Spellbook

Mana 33

Spells

0 Daze, Detect Magic, Energy Burst, Mage Hand, Read Magic

1 Burning Hands, Color Spray, Expeditious Retreat, Feather Fall, Hypnotism, Identify, Mage Armor, Silent Image

2 Aid, Alter Self, Call Element, Invisibility, Sound Burst, Whispering Wind

3 Call Lightning, Daylight, Flame Arrow, Haste, Major Image, Wind Wall

---

LORTHAIN   CR 5

Male Human Fighter 6

Size: M

Space: 5 ft. x 5 ft.

Type Humanoid (Human)

HD (6d10)+24; hp 63

Init +0 (+0 Dex, +0 Misc)

Vision AL: None

DEFENSE

AC 16 (touch 10, flatfooted 16)

Fort +8, Ref +2, Will +4

OFFENSE

Speed Walk 30 ft.

STATISTICS

STR 15, DEX 10, CON 16, INT 13, WIS 14, CHA 11

*Greatsword +2 +11/+6 S (2d6+6 19–20/x2 Both M)

Feats Blind-Fight, Cleave, Coordinated Maneuvers, Great Cleave, Power Attack, Quick Draw, Shield of Swings, Vital Strike

Skills Acrobatics −2, Climb +5, Handle Animal +4, Intimidate +9, Knowledge (Dungeoneering) +5, Knowledge (Geography) +2, Perception +5, Ride +4, Stealth −1, Survival +6, Swim +3

Special Qualities Armor Training (Ex), Bonus Feat, Bonus Feats, Bravery (Ex), Skilled, Weapon Training (Ex)

Possessions 1 Greatsword +2, 1 Breastplate

Illustration by Michael Bielaczyc

THE TOMB OF THE RESLYS

Once the adventurers' attention turns to the graveyard, it is rather easy to find the Tomb of the Reslys. The Reslys have been a part of the city for a while, and they have a personal tomb toward the back of the graveyard, butted up against a slight hill. Gret and Edna Barris, the overseers of the cemetery, will point the adventurers in the right direction. The married couple has no love for Resly and will have a gleam in their eyes as they send the adventurers into the graveyard. Behind the grave is a laboratory that Resly's father and grandfather used for nefarious purposes. Resly never liked it, preferring his hidden study in his manor. Ironically, using the study at home led to the death of his wife, which caused him to end up here, trying to resurrect her.

Read the following:

The clouds let no light down to warm the ground of this haunting place. Old tombstones, worn down to little more than rocks, dot the landscape. Others tower into the sky, intricately carved statues resembling the deceased, covered in a layer of ever present dew. You quickly move away from the cottage at the head of the graveyard; the wild haired old couple who pointed the way toward the Resly tomb still bring chills to your spine. There was just something off about them.

Beyond the graves to the south, the ground falls away to the canyon called the Dead Gulch, a resting place for those who cannot afford a tombstone or plot of land. To the north east, you can see the small hill that the Resly tomb rests in.

They encounter nothing as they traverse the graveyard, but feel free to play up a sense of fear. As they approach the hill, read the following:

The hill towers up, made taller by the flat lands around it. An iron gate with the worn name of Resly leads to a small marble building built directly into the side of the mound. Its door stands slightly ajar, and the grass around it has been worn with traffic.

A DC 20 perception check shows human footprints in and out, and a DC 25 shows other smaller claw like footprints as well.

1. THE TOMB

Four dusty caskets sit in each corner of this small tomb. The aged stone walls are damp and have pockets of moss and lichen clinging to the old bricks. In the back of the tomb is a newer stone slab, fitting flush into the wall around it.

Puzzle

Four symbols form a circle next to the stone slab, about three hands from the floor. Each has a small hole beneath the image. A metal rod hangs by a chain to its left.

Trap — DC 18 to spot (XP 100). If the wrong hole is chosen, then a small bit of powder will shoot out of a small hole above the symbols. Whoever was putting the rod in will get hit with Gravenight Spores (DC 15 reflex to dodge) and suffer a −4 to Perception for the next hour. DC 18 to disable.

The puzzle has four symbols that the boggarts in the tomb use as a key to get in. Three symbols: the dog, the fire, and the sun are all things boggarts hate. The drop of blood symbol is the correct keyhole to open the door.

Also, any wrong hole will cause a large bell to ring behind the door. If the adventurers check for dust, it is a DC 12 perception check to see that the hole with the blood drop has no dust in it.

2. THE LONG HALLWAY

The hallway in front of you is made of cut stone arching above you. The dirt floor is covered in footprints up and down the length as it slowly descends into the dark ahead.

DC 15 perception to notice both small footprints and human-sized boot prints. DC 20 shows that there has also been a high-heeled shoe as well, though there are many less tracks from it. DC 25 reveals that the tracks seem to walk very close to either side of the wall at a certain place in the tunnel, avoiding the center of the path. Also, the SG should reveal this information to any adventurer who specifically states that they follow the footprints. This will allow skilled trackers or clever players to bypass the first trap below.

Hall Trap

This is a double trap, meant to give intruders a false sense of security when they find the pit trap. A small path on either side of the pit allows the adventurers to pass easily; but if they spring the second trap, the log that swings down is the same width as the hall and will knock the first two intruders past the pit trap back into it, unless they roll a successful reflex save.

PART ONE – PIT TRAP   CR 1/2

XP 200
Type Mechanical
Perception DC 12; Disable Device DC 20
Effects Trigger location; Reset manual
Effect 10-ft-deep pit (1d6 falling damage); DC 20 Reflex avoids; multiple targets (all targets in a 10-ft-square area)

PART TWO – SWINGING LOG TRAP   CR 1

XP 300
Type Mechanical; touch trigger; manual reset
Atk +5 melee (2d6, log); Perception DC 20; Disable Device DC 20

3. THE BOGGARTS' LAIR

The room ahead is lit by a firepit in the middle of its dirt floor. Stone pillars stretch to the ceiling throughout the room. Small humanoid creatures sit around the fire, while a larger one sits on a rough wooden throne.

Door, wooden. Unlocked.

Strategy

The boggarts will hide behind the pillars and use their slings. The Lakava will run to the strongest magic user and use his ability to try and stun them, then attack the next weakest character. The chief will attack the biggest adventurer to try and show his strength to his clan.

BOGGART LAIR ENCOUNTER   CR 4

XP 1300

BOGGARTS (5)   CR 5

CR 1/4
XP 100 each
Init +3
Senses Darkvision 60 ft., Perception +4

DEFENSE
AC 17, touch 14, flat footed 14 (+2 armor, +3 dex, +1 shield, +1 size)
hp 4 (1d8)
Fort +1, Ref +4, Will −1

OFFENSE
Speed 20 ft., Climb 20 ft.
Melee Rusted Dagger +1 (1d4 −1, crit: 19–20)
Ranged Sling +5 (1d3)

LAKAVA   CR 1

The Lakava is a creature left over from one of Rosaga and Resly's experiments with bringing creatures over from the Navirim. It is quite content staying in the dark beneath the graves, serving as a guardian for Resly's hidden lab.

Small outsider
XP 400
Init +7
Senses Darkvision 60 ft., Low-Light Vision, Scent

Illustration by Christopher Burdett

DEFENSE
AC 14
hp 7 (1d8)
Fort +1, Ref +4, Will +1

OFFENSE
Speed 30 ft.
Melee Bite +2 (1d4–1), (2) Claw 1d3–1
Special Attacks Maniacal Laugh

STATISTICS
STR 9, DEX 16, CON 10, INT 10, WIS 9, CHA 8
Base Atk +2; **CMB** –1; **CMD** 10
Feats Improved Initiative
Skills Perception +5, Stealth +5
Languages Common, Demon

SPECIAL ABILITIES
Maniacal Laugh (Su) DC 12 will save or be shaken for 1d4 rounds.

BOGGART CHIEF (POSSESSED) GERSHAK   CR 1

The demon hasn't totally taken over, and the only ability Gershak has been imbued with is the ability to blend into his surroundings.

XP 400 (possessed)
Male Boggart Fighter 2
Init +3
Senses Darkvision 60 ft., Perception +1

DEFENSE
AC 20, touch 14, flat-footed 17 (+4 armor, +3 Dex, +1 natural, +1 size, +1 shield,)
hp 14 (2d10)+1
Fort +1, Ref +3, Will –1, +1 Will vs. fear

OFFENSE
Speed 20 ft.
Melee Hammer (light) (small) +6 (1d3+1)
Ranged Hammer (light) (small/thrown) +7 (1d3+1)
Melee Shield (light/wooden) (small) +1 (1d2)

SPECIAL ABILITIES
Camouflage +8 to hide, even in plain sight — Gershak is possessed by a demon of the Navirim.

HISTORY
Rosaga and Resly needed to experiment to make sure their ritual worked to bring over his wife's spirit. They found the Boggarts, who inhabited the graveyard, to be the perfect subjects. They had many failures, but Gershak was successfully possessed by a creature from the other side. With his newfound power, he quickly rose to power over the other Boggarts. The Lakava is the last experiment of the two necromancers. They successfully brought the Lakava over from the Navirim, and it possessed the infant corpse.

4. THE LABORATORY
(CR 5 Encounter XP 2200)

This room is furnished nicer than the room before, even having a couple of rugs on its hard-packed dirt floor. A small brazier in the center of the room casts its light, illuminating tables filled with flasks, bottles, and strange instruments. Around the walls of the room are many cages filled with different creatures of various sizes. At the rear of the room, a small staircase leads up to another level in which you can see a well-dressed man and woman near a table with lit candles and a still-hot meal.

**If alarm was raised, door must be kicked in; they will be barred from the other side. Strong wooden. 20 hp

Strategy
Lady Resly will fight to the death, she has no care for this body. Lord Resly will fight to the death once she is gone. Or he will kill himself with a small knife he keeps in his belt.

BOGGART ZOMBIES   CR 1/4
(One Boggart per adventurer)
XP 200 each
NE Small humanoid (goblinoid)
Init +3
Senses Darkvision 60 ft., Perception +4

DEFENSE
AC 11, touch 10, flat footed 10
hp 13 (2d8)
Fort +1, Ref +1, Will 3
DR 5/slashing

OFFENSE
Speed 20 ft., Climb 20 ft.
Melee Slam 1d4, Rusted Weapon +1 (1d4 –1, crit: 19–20)

SPECIAL ABILITIES

Staggered (Ex) Zombies have poor reflexes and can only perform a single move action or standard action each round. A zombie can move up to its speed and attack in the same round as a charge action.

GHOUL (1)   CR 1

XP 400
CE Medium undead
Init +2
Senses Darkvision 60 ft., Perception +7

DEFENSE
AC 14, touch 12, flat-footed 12 (+2 Dex, +2 natural)
hp 13 (2d8+4)
Fort +2, Ref +2, Will +5
Defensive Abilities Channel Resistance +2
Immune Undead Traits

OFFENSE
Speed 30 ft.
Melee Bite +3 (1d6+1 plus disease and paralysis) and 2 Claws +3 (1d6+1 plus paralysis)
Special Attacks Paralysis (1d4+1 rounds, Fort DC 13, elves are immune to this effect)

STATISTICS
STR 13, DEX 15, CON —, INT 13, WIS 14, CHA 14
Base Atk +1; **CMB** +2; **CMD** 14
Feats Weapon Finesse
Skills Acrobatics +4, Climb +6, Perception +7, Stealth +7, Swim +3
Languages Common

SPECIAL ABILITIES
Disease (Su) Ghoul Fever: Bite — injury; save Fort DC 13; onset 1 day; frequency 1/day; effect 1d3 Con and 1d3 Dex damage; cure 2 consecutive saves. The save DC is Charisma-based.

A humanoid who dies of ghoul fever rises as a ghoul at the next midnight. A humanoid who becomes a ghoul in this way retains none of the abilities it possessed in life. It is not under the control of any other ghouls, but it hungers for the flesh of the living and behaves like a normal ghoul in all respects. A humanoid of 4 Hit Dice or more rises as a ghast.

LORD RESLY   CR 2

XP 800
Male Human Necromancer 3
None Medium humanoid (human)
Init +4
Senses Perception +3

DEFENSE
AC 10, touch 10, flat-footed 10
hp 11 (3HD)
Fort +0, Ref +1, Will +4

OFFENSE
Speed 30 ft. (6 squares)
Space 5 ft.
Reach 5 ft.
Special Actions Power Over Undead ~ Command Undead, Prepared Spells

Mana 12

Spells *Wizard (CL 3rd)*
0 Light, Energy Orb, *Touch of Fatigue (DC 15)
1 Burning Hands (DC 16), Cause Fear (DC 16), Chill Touch (DC 16), Magic Missile
2 Burning Taze (DC 17), Web (DC 17)

STATISTICS
STR 9, DEX 11, CON 9, INT 20, WIS 13, CHA 14
Base Atk +1; **CMB** +0; **CMD** 10
Feats Alertness, Combat Casting, Command Undead, Improved Initiative, Scribe Scroll
Skills Appraise +11, Bluff +5, Climb −1, Craft (Alchemy) +11, Craft (Untrained) +5, Diplomacy +2, Disguise +3, Heal +3, Intimidate +4, Knowledge (Arcana) +10, Knowledge (History) +9, Knowledge (Planes) +10, Knowledge (Religion) +9, Linguistics (Abyssal) +9, Perception +3, Perform (Untrained) +2, Sense Motive +3, Spellcraft +11, Survival +1, Swim −1
Languages Abyssal, Celestial, Common, Draconic, Druidic, Sylvan
Special Qualities Abjuration Opposition School, Arcane Bond, Bolster, Bonded Object, Bonus Feat, Cantrips, Necromancy School, Skilled, Transmutation Opposition School, Weapon and Armor Proficiency
Possessions Healing salve 1d6

Spellbook (Wizard's)
0 Light, Energy Orb, Touch of Fatigue
1 Cause Fear, Chill Touch, Magic Missile
2 Burning Gaze, Ghoul Touch, Web

LADY RESLY

CR 2

Sirin
XP 600
LE Medium outsider
Init +3
Senses Darkvision 60 ft., Detect Opposing, Detect Magic, See in Darkness; Perception +7

DEFENSE

AC 17, touch 16, flat-footed 13 (+3 Dex, +1 dodge, +1 natural, +2 size)
hp 12 (3d6); Fast Healing 2
Fort +1, Ref +6, Will +4
DR 5/iron or silver
Immune Cold, Poison
Resist Acid 10

OFFENSE

Speed 20 ft., fly 50 ft. (perfect)
Melee Claw +6 (1d4), Claw +6 (1d4)
Space 2–1/2 ft.
Reach 0 ft.
Spell-Like Abilities (CL 6th)
- Constant — Detect Opposing, Detect Magic
- At will — Cloudform (leaving body behind)
- 1/day — Augury, Suggestion (DC 15)

STATISTICS

STR 10, DEX 17, CON 10, INT 13, WIS 12, CHA 14
Base Atk +3; **CMB** +1; **CMD** 15
Feats Dodge, Weapon Finesse
Skills Acrobatics +9, Bluff +8, Fly +21, Knowledge (arcana) +7, Knowledge (planes) +7, Perception +7, Spellcraft +7
Languages Common, Naviri

SPECIAL ABILITIES

Ear-Piercing Scream (DC 14 Fort) (4 times per day) A powerful scream, inaudible to all but a single target. The target is dazed for 1 round and takes 1d6 points of sonic damage per two caster levels (maximum 5d6). A successful save negates the daze effect and halves the damage.

> **Casting Time** 1 standard action
> **Components** V, S
> **Effect**
> - **Range** close (25 ft. + 5 ft./2 levels)
> - **Target** one creature
> - **Duration** instantaneous; see text
> - **Saving Throw** Fortitude partial (see text); Spell Resistance yes

ECOLOGY

Environment Any
Organization Solitary, pair
Treasure Standard

HISTORY

Resly knows that he was unsuccessful in raising his wife, but he is blinded by grief and the fact that his wife's body is inhabited by some glimmer of life once again. While he dallied with many other women during his marriage, when he lost his wife, he realized how much he still desired her.

He has been unsuccessfully trying to win the Sirin's attention, offering food and wine. The Sirin is using him and his madness to rest after her transition into this plane to regain some of her power.

The Sirin has been aiding Rosaga for years, whispering in her dreams and leading her down the path to allowing her to escape the Navirim. Rosaga knew that she could not bring back Resly's wife, but saw an opportunity to try and bring the Sirin over.

TREASURE

- Spellbook with Resly's Spells
- The Journal of Resly — His journal reveals that he has been learning spells for quite some time. His wife found out and tried to leave him. A fight ensued, and she fell down the cellar stairs to her death. When he looked down at her lifeless body, his first fear was for his own well being. Then slowly, as he realized he would never see his wife again, combined with his spoiled habit of wanting that which he cannot have, he began to desire her. It seems he convinced himself that he had been madly "in love" with her for all these years and didn't realize it until now. It mentions he had met someone at the circus several seasons past, who claimed to know how to bring someone back from the dead. So he went to the circus to learn how to bring his wife back to life. He refers to the person as "she," so it is definitely a female magic user. He does not refer to her by name, but does call her "R."
- 6 books about the occult, history of magic, and superstitions worth 4 gp.
- 15 gp, 56 sp.
- Ornate necklace with pearls (On Lady Resly) worth 35 gp.
- Small steel mirror worth 10 gp.
- Silver dagger worth 35 gp.
- Gold cane of Lord Resly worth 75 gp at any shop, worth 250 gp to a collector knowing its source.
- In many unbound sheets of parchment, there are various notes, illustrations, and symbols showing some strange ritual.

BACK TO THE CIRCUS

Both Belial and the notes in the grave laboratory point towards Rosaga and the circus. If the players still need a push, Malynn can leave a note requesting their help at the circus.

When they return, read the following:

Wind whips the wet raindrops into your face as you enter the circus ground. The sudden storm seems to have taken many of the patrons by surprise, and they run back and forth trying to find shelter. There is something unnatural about the weather; the clouds overhead seem to be swirling, centered above the circus. Two bolts of lightning crackle across the sky, leaving behind strange green glowing paths which slowly fade into the turbulent clouds. Ahead, you hear some patrons scream.

Rosaga is trying the ritual to revive her love, using Davin as the recipient body. She has charmed her audience to use their life energy for the ritual; but her spell was not strong enough, and some of them resisted and escaped. They now run from the tent screaming of witchcraft and sorcery. As the adventurers watch, a green bolt of lightning strikes the center of the Big Top lighting it on fire. With all of this happening, the cries of the patrons leaving Rosaga's tent seem unnoticed to any but the adventurers.

Battle Strategy

Screaming patrons run from the tent; Rosaga has taken some patrons prisoner. She is planning on using one as a body for the Siren. Malynn is there as well as Lorthain. They get trapped in a potion web trap thrown by Rosaga. Rosaga runs, leaving her daughter to fight. The patrons, under the control of Rosaga, attack the adventurers with their fists. The skeletons that appeared to just add ambiance to the tent have begun to move. They attack the adventurers, who notice they have an eerie green glow about them. Anva fights and tries to continue the ritual. A skeleton holds back the youngest daughter, who is crying, shocked by the revelation of what her family truly is. Without Rosaga, the ritual fails, somewhat. When Anva finishes chanting, she stabs Davin (if the adventurers do not stop her). After a few moments, Davin rises, his eyes blank. The spirit of the Sirin flies around the battle and distracts the adventurers. It is incorporeal, so it can not attack, nor can it be hit.

Malynn frees himself, pausing only to tell the adventurers that he and Lorthain are going after Rosaga.

The patrons will only slow the adventurers. If the adventurers kill any of the patrons, they will have Cameron and the City Guard to answer to.

PATRONS (6)   CR 1/2
XP 200
Human Commoner 1/Expert 1
N Medium humanoid
Init +0
Senses Perception +1

DEFENSE
AC 10, touch 10, flat-footed 10
hp 4
Fort +1, Ref +0, Will +3

OFFENSE
Speed 30 ft.
Melee Club +0 (1d6)

MEDIUM SKELETONS (5)   CR 1/3
XP 135
NE Medium undead
Init +6
Senses Darkvision 60 ft., Perception +0

DEFENSE
AC 16, touch 12, flat-footed 14 (+2 armor, +2 Dex, +2 natural)
hp 4 (1d8)
Fort +0, Ref +2, Will +2
DR 5/bludgeoning
Immune Cold, Undead Traits

OFFENSE
Speed 30 ft.
Melee Broken Scimitar +0 (1d6), Claw −3 (1d4+1) or 2 Claws +2 (1d4+2)

STATISTICS
STR 15, DEX 14, CON —, INT —, WIS 10, CHA 10
Base Atk +0; **CMB** +2; **CMD** 14
Feats Improved Initiative
Gear Broken Chain Shirt, Broken Scimitar

DAVIN (ZOMBIE)

CR 1

XP 200
NE Medium undead
Init +0
Senses Darkvision 60 ft.; Perception +0

DEFENSE

AC 12, touch 10, flat-footed 12 (+2 natural)
hp 27
Fort +0, Ref +0, Will +3
DR 5/slashing
Immune Undead Traits

OFFENSE

Speed 30 ft.
Melee Slam +4 (1d6+4)

STATISTICS

STR 17, DEX 10, CON —, INT —, WIS 10, CHA 10
Base Atk +1; **CMB** +4; **CMD** 14
Feats Toughness
Special Qualities Staggered

SPECIAL ABILITIES

Staggered (Ex) Zombies have poor reflexes and can only perform a single move action or standard action each round. A zombie can move up to its speed and attack in the same round as a charge action.

ANVA

CR 1

Anva is worn out from the ritual. She will not put up a fight, unless the adventurers push her. She will use the last bit of her spells to try and slow down the adventurers and escape.

XP 400
Female Human Enchanter 2
None Medium humanoid (human)
Init +1
Senses Perception +0

DEFENSE

AC 11, touch 11, flat-footed 10 (+1 Dex)
hp 13 (2d6+1)
Fort −1, Ref +1, Will +3

OFFENSE

Speed 30 ft.
Melee dagger +0 (1d4−1/19–20)
Ranged Dagger (thrown) +2 (1d4/19–20)

Special Attacks Dazing Touch
Spells *Wizard (CL 2nd, concentration +4)*
0 (at will) Acid Splash, Bleed (DC 13)
1 Charm Person (DC 14), Hypnotism (DC 14), Obscuring Mist

STATISTICS

STR 9, DEX 13, CON 9, INT 16, WIS 10, CHA 16
Base Atk +1; **CMB** +0; **CMD** 11
Feats Combat Casting, Scribe Scroll, Toughness
Skills Appraise +7 , Bluff +5 , Craft (Calligraphy) +7, Diplomacy +5 , Intimidate +5 , Knowledge (Arcana) +7 , Knowledge (Planes) +7 , Spellcraft +7
Languages Common, Sylvan
Special Qualities Bonus Feat, Bonus Wizard Spell, Cantrips, Enchanting Smile, Skilled
Gear Dagger, Spellbook (Wizard's)

Spellbook (Wizard's)
0 Acid Splash, Bleed
1 Charm Person, Hypnotism, Obscuring Mist

SPECIAL ABILITIES

Cantrips You can prepare a number of cantrips, or 0-level spells, each day. These spells are cast like any other spell, but they are not expended when cast and may be used again. You can prepare a cantrip from a prohibited school, but it uses up two of your available slots.

Dazing Touch (Sp) You can cause a living creature to become dazed for 1 round as a melee touch attack. Creatures with more than 2 hit dice are unaffected. You may use this ability 6 times per day.

Enchanting Smile (Su) You gain a +2 enhancement bonus on Bluff, Diplomacy, and Intimidate skill checks.

After the battle, Malynn returns. Rosaga is chained and wearing what is called an Iron Grin, a metal device that wraps around the head, holding the mage's mouth open so they cannot speak. A set of chains hang down and lock the thumbs together. If the players did not kill Anva, Malynn will also chain her in an Iron Grin and take her away. He will task the players to chase down the Sirin. If they trap the spirit, or the body it inhabits, within a circle of salt, the creature can no longer flee to another host. Then a silver dagger to its heart, while trapped, can send it back to the Navirim. Malynn must deal with Rosaga. She is too powerful to leave unattended, and Malynn believes the adventurers are strong enough to get rid of the Sirin. He will even give them a silver dagger, inscribed in runes to banish the creature.

Aftermath in the Circus

Davin could be dead; Rosaga and her daughter are prisoners of a Tower Mage, and the unnatural storm destroyed many of the circus tents. Olesya will back up the adventurer's stories, as long as they tell the truth. The City Guard are not as concerned about the circus as they are the patrons from Ferryport. Spend as much or as little time as you want to play out the aftermath of the battle. After the battle, the SG can reveal the plans to the adventurers through notes and a journal of Rosaga's, or Anva can break down and answer questions from Malynn and the adventurers. Rosaga will say nothing, but Anva will tell about the history with her father, their experiments on the road, and the deal with the being from the Never.

Optional Encounter — The Mob

After the battle in the tent, many patrons and locals have arrived to investigate the strange clouds and lighting. While Malynn is chasing after Rosaga, the adventurers are confronted by the other members of the Circus and the locals. The situation gets heated and can easily become an angry mob. A DC 20 diplomacy check while explaining those questioning will placate them, but the Story Guide should really play up the fact that they may get blamed for this. They have quite a bit to explain; but if they are honest, the crowd will calm down.

The Funeral of Lord Resly

Lord Resly has died, but it seems only the adventurers know the truth. When they arrive back to see Tain, he informs them that they are invited, along with Tain and Silas, to the funeral of Lord Resly. Tain is just as confused as the adventurers. The letter stated that Resly and his wife were ambushed by bandits traveling back from Garaden, and both perished in the attack. Tain suggests they should attend with him and Silas.

At the funeral, the adventurers are approached by Belial. He seems to be in charge at the wake, which is taking place at the Resly Manor. He makes small talk and mentions that it is a shame that Resly met such "an unfortunate end." He says he is quite interested in the story behind what really happened at the Circus; and at some future point they should meet for tea. He also says that maybe he would need the services of such a resourceful group of people sometime in the future.

LEVELING UP

The adventurers will have gathered enough XP at this point to level up, and this is the first break which would give them time to train, meditate, and study enough to level. They have many options for mentoring: Tain and Malynn for magic users, Jirrim or Guardsman Garamond for melee as examples.

They can continue their search for the Sirin, as well as visit shops or other places to restock or buy needed equipment while also training.

"I am tired of running into all these damn gerblins and boggers."

Agnar at the Southgate Inn after quite a few meads

THE DEAD GULCH

FINDING THE SIRIN

You have found Lord Resly and attended his funeral. You helped Malynn imprison Rosaga the Seer for her involvement in her family's dark plans. But now, all eyes are on Tain and Silas after the death of Resly; and Malynn has gone to the East to deliver Rosaga to the Tower. You were left to find the escaped Sirin, a Fey from the Navirim, who is likely to cause problems for the people of Ferryport.

For a week, you searched with no luck; but now a freak storm has erupted over the cemetery, with the same swirling clouds and green light you saw at the Circus. You grab the jars of salt and the silver dagger that Malynn left, and you head out into the gray day to find a demon.

THE CEMETERY

Read the following:

As you approach the cemetery, a storm has gathered. Rain flies sideways in the strong wind, and the clouds swirl into an unnatural vortex of green light above the canyon beyond the graveyard. Lightning strikes down to the cliff sides on either side of the Dead Gulch, the rocks scorched black. If the Sirin is anywhere, she would be there, deep in the caves below.

THE DEAD GULCH

The smell is overwhelming. The Dead Gulch was used as a mass grave for the poor souls who died of the plagues. Even though a body or two may be found dumped in the gulch these days, it is mainly used as a place to dispose of trash. When it rains, the canyon fills with water and the trash is washed deep into the cavern at the far end of the gulch.

It has been raining for days, so there is not as much refuse as there could be. The Sirin fled here, drawn by a crossroad and the undead created by Rosaga and Resly. Over the years, Rosaga and Resly have raised some failed experiments, and they have congregated here. The Sirin found the discarded corpse of a lady of the night and possessed that body. She fled deep into the caverns and there immediately opened a rift to the Navirim and began to bring her brethren over to inhabit the many corpses and skeletons found deep in the cavern.

1. THE CAVERN

Past the canyon, you find a large cavern. The cave narrows quickly, its walls smooth from erosion, but then opens into a much larger cavern. The floor is slick with mud, and trash is embedded throughout. The floor angles down toward the middle of the room, and water moves slowly to a larger pool to one side. It is pitch black inside the cave.*

* From here on, except for the Boggart hideout and the final room, some sort of light is needed.

As the characters traverse the slick floor, zombies begin to rise from the muddiest parts. They are some of the first experiments of Rosaga and Resly, and are decomposed and completely unintelligent. The adventurers must succeed at a DC 15 perception check or be caught flat-footed by the zombies. They will rise right next to the adventurers and start grabbing ankles and legs. To fight on this slick surface, each character must make a DC 12 Reflex save or fall over. The zombies do not have to make this check because they move so slowly. If the adventurers move to the area near the water, which has a steeper downhill slope, the Zombies must make the reflex save to follow.

ZOMBIE (5)   CR 1/2
(Arrive in waves)

XP 200 each
NE Medium undead
Init +0
Senses Darkvision 60 ft.; Perception +0

DEFENSE
AC 12, touch 10, flat-footed 12 (+2 natural)
hp 12 (2d8+3)
Fort +0, Ref +0, Will +3
DR 5/slashing
Immune Undead Traits

OFFENSE
Speed 30 ft.
Melee Slam +4 (1d6+4)

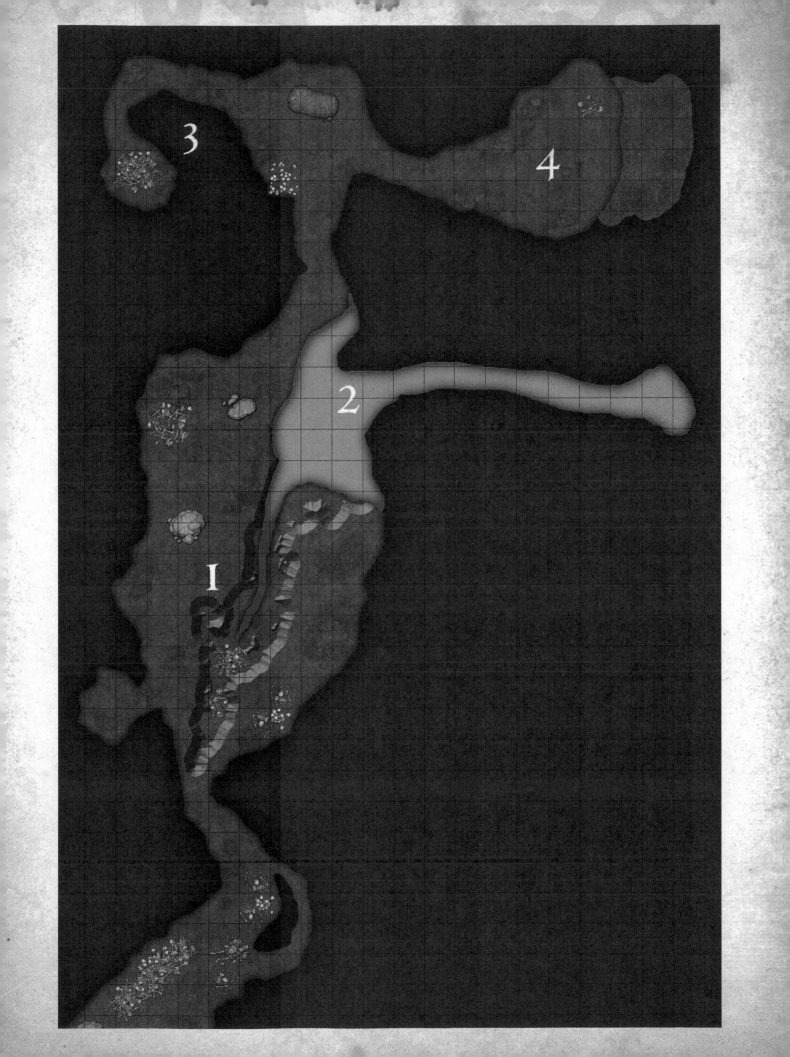

Illustration by Christopher Burdett

STATISTICS
STR 17, DEX 10, CON —, INT —, WIS 10, CHA 10
Base Atk +1; **CMB** +4; **CMD** 14
Feats Toughness
Special Qualities Staggered

SPECIAL ABILITIES
Staggered (Ex) Zombies have poor reflexes and can only perform a single move action or standard action each round (it has the staggered condition.) A zombie can move up to its speed and attack in the same round as a charge action.

2. THE STREAM
This stream flows out from the mud and down a narrow passage. At the end, there is a drop off; and you can hear the water crashing below.

The passage is 4' wide and 3' tall, meaning to travel down the stream, the adventurers must do it on their bellies in cold water. There is no way for the adventurers to tell how far the waterfall is at the end, but there is not enough current to push anyone over who doesn't want to go.

Waterfall — 15' into a small underground pond which is 10 feet deep under the falls. DC 15 Reflex to not bang against the rocks on the way down, which would cause 1d4 damage.

3. LAIR OF THE TENTACLE CRAWLER
A Tentacle Crawler will emerge and attack, backing the players toward the cliff.

TENTACLE CRAWLER   CR 4
A tentacle crawler looks like a giant centipede with five octopus-like tentacles emerging from its head. It roams the darkness in search of prey, using its tentacles to grapple it while it stings with its barbed tail.

XP 1200
N Huge vermin
Init +0
Senses Darkvision 60 ft.; Perception +5

DEFENSE
AC 18, touch 10, flat footed 16 (+8 natural armor, −2 size, +2 dex)

hp 42 (5d8 +20)
Fort +11, Ref +2, Will +1
Immune Mind-affecting effects

OFFENSE
Speed 40 ft., Climb 40 ft.
Melee Bite +8 (1d6+9 plus grab), tail sting +8 (1d6+9 plus poison)
Space 10 ft.
Reach 10 ft.
Special Attacks Constrict (1d4+6), Poison

STATISTICS
STR 28, DEX 14, CON 19, INT —, WIS 11, CHA 2
Base Atk +3; **CMB** +14; **CMD** 25 (can't be tripped)
Skills Climb +12, Perception +5, Stealth +1; Racial Modifiers +6 Climb, +3 Perception, +8 Stealth

SPECIAL ABILITIES
Poison (Ex) Sting — injury; save Fort DC 16; frequency 1/round for 6 rounds; effect 1d3 Strength damage; cure 1 save. The save DC is Constitution-based and includes a +2 racial bonus.

Grab If the tentacle crawler successfully lands a bite attack, it deals 1d6+9 damage, and using its tentacles, attempts to start a grapple as a free action without provoking an attack of opportunity. It may only grab Large or smaller opponents. The crawler has the option to conduct the grapple normally or simply use its claw to hold the opponent. If it chooses to do the latter, it takes a −20 penalty on its CMB check to make and maintain the grapple, but does not gain the grappled condition itself. A successful hold does not deal any extra damage.

ECOLOGY
Environment Subterranean, sewer, swamp
Organization Solitary

TREASURE
- Gems (760 gp)
  - Aquamarine (worth 300 gp)
  - Black pearl (worth 200 gp)
  - Jet (worth 130 gp)
  - Tourmaline (worth 130 gp)
- Wondrous item (5200 gp) — Circlet of Comprehend Languages and Read Magic (worth 5200 gp) — This ancient circlet was crafted by the Mages of the West. During the last age, one of them must have died nearby, his corpse washing down into the Gulch. His skeleton and other items long lost, the silver crown lodged itself back in the lair of the tentacle crawler.

4. CAVERN CLIFF

The floors drops off into the darkness below. The cliff leading down is slick with water and mud, but there look to be many foot and handholds.

CLIFF

DC 20 to climb. 40' Drop — 3d6 damage if a character slips from the top

5. THE ZOMBIE CAVE

The cave opens up before you into a large chamber. Your light illuminates only the small part which you occupy. The ground here is muddy, but not as muddy as before. But you hear the tell-tale signs of something sloshing ahead of you. Green glowing eyes can be seen in the darkness, slowly approaching. As you ready your weapons, something else moves, something higher in the chamber. As you ready your weapons, something swoops down, its flesh red and raw, and its wings batlike. A wicked smile splits its face revealing a multitude of needle-like teeth.

ZOMBIES (3)

(same stats as zombies in area 1, page 42)

IMP   CR 2

XP 600

LE Tiny outsider (devil, evil, extraplanar, lawful)
Init +3
Senses Darkvision 60 ft., Detect Good, Detect Magic, See in Darkness; Perception +7

DEFENSE

AC 17, touch 16, flat-footed 13 (+3 Dex, +1 dodge, +1 natural, +2 size)
hp 16 (3d10); Fast Healing 2
Fort +1, Ref +6, Will +4
DR 5/good or silver
Immune Fire, Poison
Resist Acid 10, Cold 10

OFFENSE

Speed 20 ft., fly 50 ft. (perfect)
Melee Sting +8 (1d4 plus poison)
Space 2–1/2 ft.
Reach 0 ft.

Spell-Like Abilities (CL 6th)
- Constant — Detect Good, Detect Magic
- At will — Invisibility (self only)
- 1/day — Augury, Suggestion (DC 15)
- 1/week — Commune (6 questions, CL 12th)

STATISTICS

STR 10, DEX 17, CON 10, INT 13, WIS 12, CHA 14
Base Atk +3; **CMB** +1; **CMD** 15
Feats Dodge, Weapon Finesse
Skills Acrobatics +9, Bluff +8, Fly +21, Knowledge (arcana) +7, Knowledge (planes) +7, Perception +7, Spellcraft +7
Languages Common, Infernal
Special Qualities Change Shape (boar, giant spider, rat, or raven, Beast Shape I)

SPECIAL ABILITIES

Poison (Ex) Sting — injury; save Fort DC 13; frequency 1/round for 6 rounds; effect 1d2 Dex; cure 1 save. The save DC is Constitution-based, and includes a +2 racial bonus.

6. THE CORPSES

The smell in this room is overpowering. Trash, rotting bodies, and bones litter every available space. But in the far corner, something small glitters on top of one of the trash piles.

While most of the refuse and corpses wash down into the underground stream and disappear deep into the gorge, this room has stopped its fair share and now sits in filth and ruin. An Otyugh has a lair here, staying away from the Boggarts and other things, enjoying the piles of filth it lives in. It will attack if something enters its den, but it will not pursue. It collects anything shiny and stacks it up along the far wall.

When half the group has entered into the room, a metal gate crashes down, splitting them in half! The Otyugh attacks those in the room, feeling threatened. If he becomes badly injured, he will flee down the tunnel and try to hide in a hollowed out nook. The pathway ends in a pile of rocks, blocking any further travel.

GATE TRAP

DC 30 to spot. DC 25 to disable.

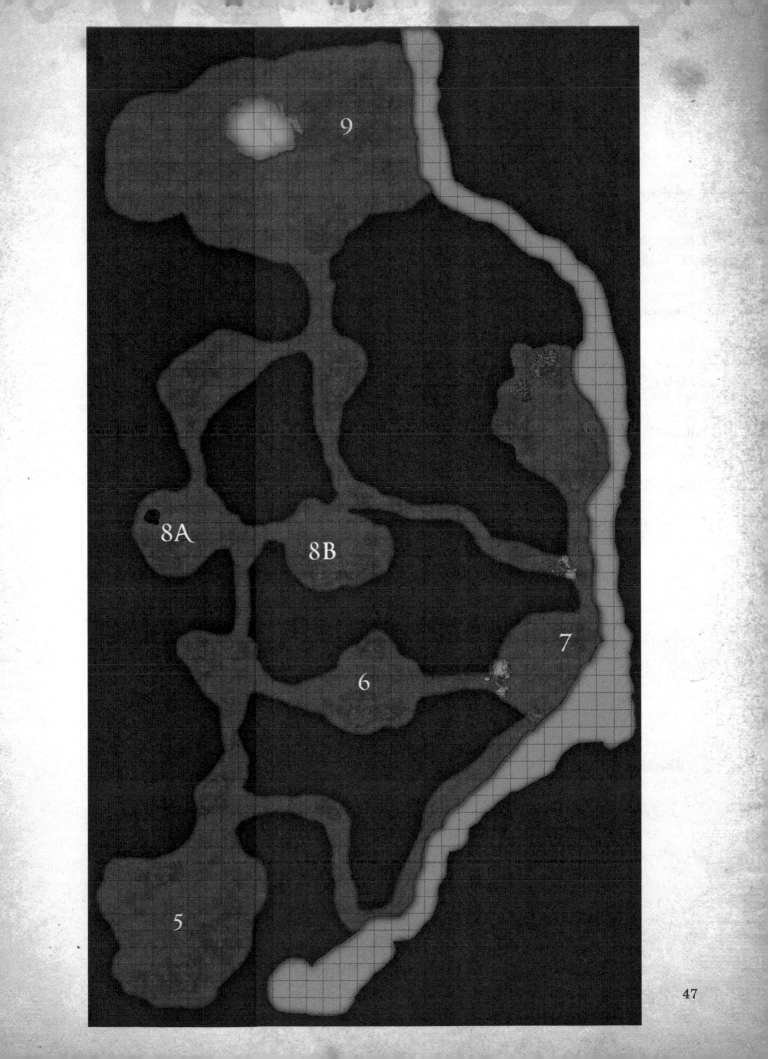

OTYUGH   CR 4

This three-legged freak is mostly mouth. Three
tentacles, two tipped with barbs and one with eyes,
extend from its sides.

XP 1,200
N Large aberration
Init +0
Senses Darkvision 60 ft., Scent; Perception +9

DEFENSE

AC 17, touch 9, flat-footed 17 (+8 natural, −1 size)
hp 39 (6d8+12)
Fort +3, Ref +2, Will +6
Immune Disease

OFFENSE

Speed 20 ft.
Melee Bite +7 (1d8+4 plus disease), 2 tentacles +3
(1d6+2 plus grab)
Space 10 ft.
Reach 10 ft. (15 ft. with tentacle)
Special Attacks Constrict (tentacle, 1d6+2)

STATISTICS

Str 18, Dex 10, Con 13, Int 5, Wis 13, Cha 6
Base Atk +4; **CMB** +9 (+13 grapple); **CMD** 19 (21
vs. trip)
Feats Alertness, Toughness, Weapon Focus (tentacle)
Skills Perception +9, Stealth +2 (+10 in lair); Racial
Modifiers +8 Stealth in lair
Languages Common

SPECIAL ABILITIES

Disease (Ex) Filth Fever: Bite — injury; save
Fortitude DC 14; onset 1d3 days; frequency 1/day;
effect 1d3 Dex damage and 1d3 Con damage; cure
2 consecutive saves. The save DC is Constitution-
based.

TREASURE (if the adventurers spend 20 minutes
sifting through the refuse)

• Gold (87 gp)
  • 54 gp
  • 330 sp
• Gems (680 gp)
  • Alexandrite (worth 500 gp)
  • Chrysoprase (worth 30 gp)
  • Onyx (worth 40 gp)
  • Pink pearl (worth 110 gp)

7. BOGGART LAIR

*The long hallway in front of you seems well traveled. Small
clawed footprints run up and down the path.*

Midway down the path is a pit trap.

SPIKED PIT TRAP   CR 2

XP 600
Type Mechanical; Perception DC 20; Disable Device
DC 20
10-ft-deep pit (1d6 falling damage); pit spikes (Atk
+10 melee, 1d4 spikes per target for 1d4+2 damage
each); DC 20 Reflex avoids; multiple targets (all
targets in a 10-ft-square area)
Effects Trigger Location; Reset Manual

---

*Ahead of you is a rough stone wall. It looks to have been
quickly erected, with a large wooden door. Small holes shine
with light, and bones are tossed everywhere as if to warn off
any intruders. As you approach, an arrow bounces off the wall.
A shrill voice shouts something from behind the door.*

The Boggarts here have been chased into hiding
by the arrival of the Sirin and have erected rough
walls for protection from the zombies and her.
They will try to banter with any adventurers; and
if anyone can speak Goblin, they can understand.
If the adventurers successfully check with a DC
18 Diplomacy, the Boggarts will tell all about the
Sirin and how to sneak into her lair through the
underground river.

If the adventurers fight, then they will have to
contend with the whole tribe, which will attack from
behind the stone wall.

BOGGARTS (14)   CR 1/4

Init +3
Senses: Darkvision 60 ft., Perception +4

DEFENSE

AC 17, touch 14, flat footed 14 (+2 armor, +3 dex,
+1 shield, +1 size)
hp 4 (1d8)
Fort +1, Ref +4, Will −1

OFFENSE

Speed 20 ft., Climb 20 ft.
Melee Rusted Dagger +1 (1d4 −1, crit: 19–20)
Ranged Shortbow +5 (1d6 −1)

Illustration by Robert Skotak

TREASURE

- Gold
  - 79 gp
  - 127 sp
  - 345 cp
- Mundane items (2 gp)
  - Crowbar (worth 2 gp)
  - Rations
  - Arrows (25)

8. TWIN CAVERNS — THE REJECTS

The tunnel branches off into two caverns here, both almost identical in size and shape.

8A. LEFT CAVERN

In this cavern, strands hang down from the ceiling, shimmering in your light. The floor shimmers, moisture clinging to all surfaces.

GLIMMER WORM   CR 2

XP 600
N Medium vermin
Init +1
Senses Darkvision 60 ft., Perception +0

DEFENSE

AC 15, touch 11, flat-footed 14 (+1 Dex, +4 natural)
hp 38
Fort +6, Ref +0, Will +1
Immune Mind-affecting effects

OFFENSE

Speed 15 ft., climb 20 ft.
Melee 1 Bite +5 (1d8+3)
Ranged Ooze +3 (slow)
Special Attacks Ooze, Slow — Adventurers move at half speed unless they successfully save vs DC 18 –STR through a space covered in Glimmer Worm's ooze. A glimmer worm may also launch a glob of ooze at its prey, which causes another save or be slowed.

STATISTICS

Str 17, Dex 12, Con 17, Int —, Wis 10, Cha 4
Base Atk +2; **CMB** +5 (+9 with pull); **CMD** 16 (28 vs. trip)
Skills Climb +11

50

ECOLOGY

Environment Any underground
Organization Solitary, pair, or tangle (3–6)
Treasure None

SPECIAL ABILITIES

Ooze (Ex) A glimmer worm can fire a small ball of slime as a standard action. This touch attack has a range of 60 feet and no range increment. A creature struck by a glimmer worm's ooze becomes stuck and is slowed to half normal speed. As a standard action, a creature can remove the slime with a DC 20 Strength check.

The glimmer worm is a specialized predator that dwells in caves. The creature's mode of hunting is unique — it clambers up a cave wall to settle on a ledge or in a crack. It coats the floors of its cave in ooze which then slows the prey down. Collections of bones and a thin coating of slime are sure signs of glimmer worm.

A glimmer worm produces its ooze from glands in its body. The glimmer worms glands can be harvested and sold to potion makers and alchemists for 40 gp.

A glimmer worm is 9 feet long and weighs 300 pounds.

8B. RIGHT CAVERN

This cavern sits empty, rising slightly in level and being a little less muddy.

HUMAN ZOMBIE (DEAD ADVENTURER)   CR 1

XP: 400
NE Medium undead
Init +0
Senses Darkvision 60 ft., Perception +0

DEFENSE

AC 12, touch 10, flat-footed 12 (+2 natural)
hp 22 (4d8+4)
Fort +1, Ref +1, Will +4
DR 5/slashing
Immune Undead Traits

OFFENSE

Speed 30 ft.
Melee Masterwork Bastard Sword +7 (1d10+3/19–20), Slam +1 (1d6+1) or Slam +6 (1d6+4)

Space 5 ft.
Reach 5 ft.

STATISTICS

STR 17, DEX 10, CON —, INT —, WIS 10, CHA 10
Base Atk +3; **CMB** +6; **CMD** 16
Feats Toughness
Special Qualities Staggered

TREASURE

- Bastard sword, the Greynotch, masterwork, possible legacy weapon

9. THE OLD BOGGART CAVERN — BONE ROOM

A large cavern opens up before you, dimly lit by a strange green pool in the center of the room. Bones are scattered about in abundance, some have even been used to create totems and grotesque furniture. From the pillared ceiling hang shrouds and totems of bones, leathered flesh and stones. There is something about the room that makes you feel sick to the pit of your stomach; but you also feel energized, as if something otherworldly is here. Among the bones, rotting corpses, covered in green liquid, wander about.

In the back of the cavern, behind the green pool, stands a large stone monolith with strange runes inscribed upon it. In front of the stone, a pale-skinned woman, dressed in the silks of a lady of the night, seems to float in mid-air. Her hands and arms are covered in blood, and you notice a fresh boggart corpse lying at her feet. Two thin streams of blood run down from her pouty lips. Her eyes are covered by a silken shroud.

This room has a ley line running through it. Magic is stronger at ley lines, and the veil between the Navirim and Uteria is a little thinner. Each adventurer who uses mana immediately gains their bonus mana on top of any mana they currently have. This only occurs in this room and can only happen once per 24 hours.

The Sirin: She has grown more powerful since she escaped the body of Lady Resly. Her dark spirit was drawn to the Dead Gulch, and there she found the discarded corpse of a woman who was killed on suspicion of being a witch. This woman, who had been a lady of the night in Fish Town (the poor quarter of Ferryport), was found with totems and strange markings in her domicile. The patron she was entertaining declared her a witch, and a mob formed taking her from the brothel, burning her eyes so she could charm no one, and cast her

into the river where she drowned. Her fellow ladies pulled her body from the river and deposited her in the Gulch, unsure if they could become cursed themselves.

This violent death attracted the energy of the Sirin, who took over the body soon after it was discarded. Now, near this ley line, she is at full power. She has been bringing over spirits to inhabit the abundant corpses in the Gulch and has even successfully brought over two beings directly from the Navirim (the Imp and the Dretches).

9A. BONE FENCE ENTRANCE

Sharp bones are stacked and tied to form a fence, only allowing one adventurer to enter at a time.

9B. RIVER ENTRANCE

If the adventurers enter from the underground river, they have a chance to surprise the Sirin. The zombies and skeletons will all be near the entrance, while the dretch will be near the green pool.

SKELETON HORDE (6)   CR 1

XP 30 each
hp 3
AC 8
Attack: Claw −2 (1d2 damage)

Hordes are groups of low level creatures that hinder adventurers due to their numbers. They often don't do much damage (though for low level characters they may), and often just slow them down as larger, more powerful creatures get to attack.

Horde Initiative

The Horde rolls initiative for each horde group. A horde group is a group attacking a single target or a gathered group of targets.

Horde Bonus

Each successive creature that attacks an adventurer gets a +1 to their attack roll. Flanking rules also apply, so characters who fight back to back or against a wall will be more defensible. If two or more characters are fighting back to back, then the cumulative bonus builds up over all surrounding "hordlings".

ZOMBIES (4) CR 1/2

XP 200
NE Medium undead
Init +0
Senses Darkvision 60 ft., Perception +0

DEFENSE
AC 12, touch 10, flat-footed 12 (+2 natural)
hp 12 (2d8+3)
Fort +0, Ref +0, Will +3
DR 5/slashing
Immune Undead Traits

OFFENSE
Speed 30 ft.
Melee Slam +4 (1d6+4)

STATISTICS
STR 17, DEX 10, CON —, INT —, WIS 10, CHA 10
Base Atk +1; **CMB** +4; **CMD** 14
Feats Toughness
Special Qualities Staggered

SPECIAL ABILITIES
   Staggered (Ex) Zombies have poor reflexes and
can only perform a single move action or standard
action each round. A zombie can move up to its speed
and attack in the same round as a charge action.

DRETCH CR 2

(1 at start of encounter, +1 Dretch every round in
which the Sirin is uninterrupted)

XP 600
CE Small outsider (chaotic, demon, evil, extraplanar)
Init +0
Senses Darkvision 60 ft., Perception +5

DEFENSE
AC 14, touch 11, flat-footed 14 (+3 natural, +1 size)
hp 18 (2d10+7)
Fort +5, Ref +0, Will +3
DR 5/cold iron or good
Immune Electricity, Poison
Resist Acid 10, Cold 10, Fire 10

OFFENSE
Speed 20 ft.
Melee 2 claws +4 (1d4+1), bite +4 (1d4+1)

Spell-Like Abilities (CL 2nd)
• 1/day — Cause Fear (DC 11), Stinking Cloud
   (DC 13), Summon (level 1, 1 dretch 35%)

STATISTICS
STR 12, DEX 10, CON 14, INT 5, WIS 11, CHA 11
Base Atk +2; **CMB** +2; **CMD** 12
Feats Toughness
Skills Escape Artist +5, Perception +5, Stealth +9
Languages Abyssal (cannot speak); Telepathy 100 ft.
(limited to Abyssal-speaking targets)

SIRIN (ESTRA'ZTH) CR 3

Medium outsider
XP 900
Init +4
Senses Darkvision 60 ft., DetectOpposing, Detect
Magic, See in Darkness; Perception +8

DEFENSE
AC 17, touch 14, flat-footed 11 (+3 Dex, +3 dodge,
+1 natural)
hp 24 (5d6); fast healing 2
Fort +1, Ref +7, Will +4
DR 5/cold iron or silver
Immune Fire, Poison
Resist Acid 10, Cold 10

OFFENSE
Speed 30 ft., Fly 50 (Out-of-body in incorporeal form)
Melee: Claw +7 (1d4+1), Claw +7 (1d4+1)
Space 5 ft.
Reach 5 ft.
Spell-Like Abilities (CL 6th)
• Constant — Detect Opposing, Detect Magic
• At will — Cloudform
• 1/day — Augury, Suggestion (DC 15)

STATISTICS
STR 10, DEX 17, CON 10, INT 13, WIS 12, CHA 14
Base Atk +3; **CMB** +1; **CMD** 15
Feats Dodge, Weapon Finesse
Skills Acrobatics +10, Bluff +8, Fly +21,
Knowledge (arcana) +7, Knowledge (planes) +7,
Perception +7, Spellcraft +7
Languages Common, Fey
Special Qualities Possess (DC12)

ECOLOGY
Environment Any
Organization Solitary, pair
Treasure Standard

SPECIAL ABILITIES
Ear-Piercing Scream (DC 16 Fort) (4 times per day) 2d6 sonic damage and daze. You unleash a powerful scream, inaudible to all but a single target. The target is dazed for 1 round and takes 1d6 points of sonic damage per two caster levels (maximum 5d6). A successful save negates the daze effect and halves the damage.

Casting Time 1 standard action
Components V, S
Effect
- **Range** close (25 ft. + 5 ft./2 levels)
- **Target** one creature
- **Duration** instantaneous; see text
- **Saving Throw** Fortitude partial (see text); Spell Resistance yes

TREASURE
- Gold (200 gp)
  - 2000 sp (worth 200 gp)
- Potions and Oils
  - Healing Salve
- Scrolls (150 gp)
  - Scroll of Ironskin

Strategy

Estra'zth, the Sirin, has recovered some of her power since the adventurers last met her. She has found this place, which seems to radiate with magical energy and is using it to call over others from the Navirim. In the battle, the skeleton horde is positioned to block intruders from the main tunnels, not the waterway. The zombies wander about in between the pool and the entrance. The Sirin is in deep concentration for her summoning, and the Dretches, small chubby demons, will surround her and try to keep her safe and uninterrupted.

Remember, the adventurers must encircle the Sirin with salt before they can destroy her spirit form, and she must be stabbed through the heart with a silver weapon in order to completely destroy her spirit. If the body is destroyed, or reaches 0 hit points, the Sirin will take gaseous form and escape. If the adventurers follow Malynn's instructions, when they pierce her heart she will scream as a green light issues from her mouth and fades as the body crumbles to the ground.

Illustration by Michael Bielaczyc

54

AFTER THE ADVENTURE

CONTACTING TAIN

After meeting up with Tain, he pays them the 10 silver each per day and takes them to Silas' manor to meet with the Guildmaster.

On the way to the manor, if the adventuring party completed their mission to Tain Northbow's satisfaction and have not done anything to get on his bad side, he will add the following:

- If they have a Wylder in their party who is interested in training as a Luminar, Tain will offer to take them under his wing and train them as a druidic luminari as described in the *Tome of the Arts: The Magic of Uteria*, which is included at the back of this adventure book.
- He would like to know if the group would be willing to enter his hire again, if any other unusual matters arise that need investigating.
- If they were particularly respectful and discreet, he will tell them how to contact him if they are in dire need of assistance.

SILAS MONTA

If the players were able to clear Monta's name, he owes them a debt of gratitude worth far more than 10 silver a day. Monta asks Tain to hand pick some minor magic items and weapons for the adventurers from his personal armory and deliver them to the party.

Some suggestions for the SG to choose from based on what their players classes are:

- **Cloak of the Forest Elves** — +3 to Stealth
- **Ancient Weapons, made from Aradan Steel** (Does not interfere with magic, +1 vs creatures of the Navirim)
  - Aradan Steel dagger
  - Aradan Steel sword
  - Aradan Steel shield
  - Aradan Steel staff
- **Ranged Weapons**
  - Masterwork crossbow
  - Masterwork bow

LEVELING UP – AWARDING EXP

Training

The characters should have met several people who are willing to train them if they played their cards right.

Enemies

The adventurers may have made some enemies who will come back to haunt them later on.

- Estra'zth — If she escapes
- Hafsha
- Fitz
- Belial Fue'vuer

Leveling

This adventure has many story driven parts, as well as combat. If the players all contributed to the story, as well as the battles, they should level from 2nd level to 4th.

IDEAS FOR FOLLOW-ON ADVENTURES

The PCs see a missing person poster in a tavern with a sketch of a woman who looks very much like the woman whose body the Sirin inhabited in the caverns.

PREGENERATED ADVENTURERS

MARAH ARARY
RANGER

Marah comes from a large family in the village of Twin Whispers, in the plains north of Ferryport. Most of her kin are farmers, though with the drought over the last years, along with raids from Unmen, farming has become a harsh in the plains.

Marah could not stand a life of scrounging for crops in the infertile soil while guarding belongings from raiders or worse. Instead, she set out to wander and find her riches. She hopes to one day return home with enough gold to move her family to more civilized lands.

Marah is average in height and build, but her striking looks often draw unwanted attention. She wears her weapons openly and proudly, often discouraging any from pushing their luck.

Since the last adventure, she has grown a little withdrawn, perhaps from spending so much time in the city. She has grown close to Jorish and Xyla, becoming protective over them.

How to Play Marah (optional)

Marah is tough, but very friendly. She will drink, jest, and arm wrestle with the best of them, but her loyalty is unwavering. If she finds companions that she holds dear, she will travel over mountain and sea to be by their side when needed.

Legacy Item

When Marah left home, her younger brother gave her his hunting bow. She prizes the bow over all other possessions, as a reminder of her home.

XYLA XIBBADOBBLER SWIFTDIGIT III
ROGUE

Xyla is an elfling, and has just left the Vale on her Calling. Since she has met the other adventurers, she now considers them her "tribe" and loyally follows them on any adventure.

To outsiders, Xyla may be similar to any other elfling, but among her people, she is a radiant beauty. Her laugh and smile disarm many she speaks with, but she is also vicious if provoked.

Since the last adventure, Xyla has become enamored with all her companions. She loves adventure, and she feels that she belongs with these people. They are her tribe.

How to play Xyla (optional)

Xyla is searching for companions to travels the lands during her Calling. She doesn't care for treasure, but at the same time, has little respect for the treasures of others. She will see no problem borrowing a companion's elven dagger to crack open a stone in search of shiny crystals.

She, like all elfings, abhors violence, and will try to find ways around fighting. Her revulsion toward creatures who torture, defile, or commit violence against her and others, however, may lead her to fight when necessary to stop their madness.

Legacy Item

Xyla's mother gave her the short sword that she had used during her Calling. While Xyla dislikes violence, a sword at her side has caused a few would be attackers to think twice about accosting the small elfling.

TORMAS ANDTRECH
FIGHTER

Tormas' father was in the Ferryport Militia when Lord Glycyn was dethroned as a traitor. His father was also implicated and was imprisoned. Tormas was unable to join the new City Guard due to his heritage. He has decided to try his luck on the road to try and bring honor and fame back to his family.

Tormas is basically a good man, though he is insecure due to his father's deception. He is tall, strong, and good looking, but also has a bit of a temper.

Since the last adventure, Tormas has opened up a little with his companions, but he is still uneasy with Jorish. With the addition of Inola and Nasir, he has been confronted with his phobias against those who are outside of his norm. He has begun to see the errors of his previous beliefs, but old habits die hard.

How to play Tormas (optional)

Tormas is searching for glory — not to make a name for himself, but to clear his family name. He is good to those around him, but can also be superstitious. He will be the first to dismiss a grand story as an old wive's tale, and he may cause problems if Jorish uses magic openly. Despite this, he is observant enough to not fall prey to his first instincts, and will judge situations with some care.

If Jorish uses magic in front of him, he may show distaste, but will not succumb to outright bigotry or confrontation. He may be distrustful of the magic, but he will not judge a person's character by what he may consider an "affliction."

Legacy Item

Tormas wears his father's scale mail armor. His father's sword was tossed into the Aerlon River with all the other weapons belonging to the "treasonous" militia; so the armor is his only inheritance.

JORISH SHAYDEN
WYLDING (MAGIC USER)

Jorish recently discovered his ability to use magic. Fearing his family's distrust of anything "supernatural," he ran away from home. He is cautious in letting others see his abilities, but is very interested in learning more of his abilities and the wizards of the past.

Jorish is tall and very skinny. Although he seems guarded, he makes friends easily and his smile tends to earn him the trust of others.

How to play Jorish (optional)

Jorish seems happy to those around him, but he lacks the confidence to let them know what secrets and misgivings he holds inside. He will do his best to hide his magical abilities unless there is no way around it. He may trust one or two members of the party with his secret, but then may internally regret it later.

Since the last adventure, Jorish has found comfort in his friendship with Marah, which has allowed him to feel more free to laugh and make jokes with the others. Jorish is conflicted about Tormas, not just because of Tormas' fear of the powers that Jorish has, but also of the physical attraction that Jorish has begun to develop for Tormas.

Legacy Item

Jorish carved a staff when he was young, and kept it hidden from his parents all these years, afraid of what they would think of it. Now that he has left home, he proudly carries it everywhere.

AGNAR
BARBARIAN

Agnar is a barbarian from the kingdom of Mideon, far to the North. When he reached the age of manhood, he went to serve in the Border Forts, but during his duty there, found no battle from which to bring himself glory. His Earl recognized his abilities and sent him south to work as a traveling mercenary, so that he might find glory in the "corrupt" southern lands.

Agnar is a stranger to these lands and cultures, but he hopes that finding adventure here will bring him coin and prestige that he can take back north.

Since the last adventure, Agnar has found himself spending time alone. He has begun to learn to work leather, but this path of self teaching is slow. The culture here seems soft to him, and he feels his companions revel in the softness, except for Marah. He sees a strength in her, but also the ability to adapt to situations that are strange to her, both of which he has great respect for. Agnar is also fearful to let the others in on his customs, which has led to him being very private. But the chance for glory and fame, he follows this group and he is happy to bring his sword along with them.

How to play Agnar (optional)

Agnar is the oldest of the companions, but he does not seek the mantle of "elder" leadership. Instead, he would prefer to follow orders while doing the best he can in the situations that present themselves. His quest for glory is not a selfish path; it is a path toward strength that also encompasses those who battle at his side.

He will be the first to rush into a battle, but he will not do so recklessly or without the consent of those with which he travels. Strength, he believes, is not found in reckless violence; it is instead found by being one with those around you and attaining victory against those who strive to hurt you or others.

Legacy Item

Agnar carries the great sword of his ancestors. If lost, he would spend his life in pursuit of it.

NASIR
SWORDSMASTER — FIGHTER

Nasir grew up in both the desert and the southern cities. His father was the tribal ruler for the el-Shiak clan. He is fourth in line to rule his clan. He has been attracted to the sword since he was young, and his father sent him off to learn more of the world, both to dull the aggressive edge of his son, and to bring back knowledge of the world outside the clan.

Nasir met Silas when he was on a diplomatic mission to South Keep, so when he began his travels he came to Silas to find employ.

How to play Nasir

Nasir is both calculating and rash. He is good at finding patterns and while he may seem to run headlong into a confrontation, he has already judged his opponents and has a plan. He is also charismatic, those around him find him a natural leader and confidant.

Legacy Item

Nasir has two swords, which he has named Bloodshed and Sorrow. While his father has always thought his son too quick to violence, Nasir is very aware of his actions. But his natural ability with weapons, especially short swords, has always held his passion.

Illustration by Sam Flegal

INOLA
DRUID — WILDE ELF (ANAVARI)

Inola came to Ferryport looking for his lost tribesman, Jyrek. When he arrived, he found that his old companion had become known as one of the new Ferryport heroes who helped dethrone the corrupt Lord Glycyn. Jyrek has left Ferryport, but many knew he was connected to Silas Monta. When Inola arrived at the manor of Silas, he had no coin, little food, and was unnerved by the strangeness of the city. Silas took him in, and Inola was introduced to the adventurers. Looking to experience what Jyrek would have experienced, he joined the adventuring group and looked to help Silas.

How to Play Inola

Inola is quiet, taking in all he can of the humans around him. He has a hard time with the human language, and an even harder time with their leanings towards violent confrontation. His interest in experiencing the new world, to see what Jyrek saw pushes him onwards.

Legacy Item

Inola has a suit of armor crafted from the scales of wyveres. His father was a famous hunter before his death, and his mother made this for his before he left on his journey. This armor acts the same as scalemail, but it does not impede his ability to cast spells.

Illustration by Sam Flegal

MARAH

Human   LVL 2
Ranger
HP: 17
AC: 15
Init: +3
base attack: +2
CMB/CMD: +3,+16
Speed: 30

ABILITIES

Str	12	
Dex	16	
Con	15	
Int	14	
Wis	10	
Cha	14	

SAVES

Fort: +5, Ref: +6, Will +0

OFFENSE

Shortbow +6 Ranged (1d6+1 / 20)
Elven LongSword +4 Melee (1d8+2 / 19-20)

SPECIAL

Favored Enemy (Evil Fey), animal Companion, Track, Wild Empathy

FEATS

Point Blank Shot, Precise Shot, Rapid Shot, Endurance

EQUIPMENT

Shortbow (Legacy), Elven Longsword, Cloak, Backpack, Rope, Sunstone (compass)

art by M. Bielaczyc

MARAH

Human   LVL 3
Ranger
HP: 26
AC: 15
Init: +3
base attack: +3
CMB/CMD: +4,+17
Speed: 30

ABILITIES

Str	12	
Dex	16	
Con	15	
Int	14	
Wis	10	
Cha	14	

SAVES

Fort: +5, Ref: +6, Will +1

OFFENSE

Shortbow +7 Ranged (1d6+1 / 20)
Elven LongSword +5 Melee (1d8+2 / 19-20)

SPECIAL

Favored Enemy (Evil Fey), animal Companion, Track, Wild Empathy

FEATS

Point Blank Shot, Precise Shot, Focused Shot, Rapid Shot, Endurance

EQUIPMENT

Shortbow (Legacy), Elven Longsword, Cloak, Backpack, Rope, Sunstone (compass)

art by M. Bielaczyc

XYLA

Elfling   LVL 2
Rogue
HP: 16
AC: 15
Init: +2
base attack: +1
CMB/CMD: +0,+12
Speed: 20

ABILITIES

Str 10
Dex 15
Con 10
Int 11
Wis 9
Cha 16

SAVES

Fort: +1, Ref: +6, Will +0

OFFENSE

Short Sword of Xandra +2 Melee (1d4 / 19-20)
Quarterstaff +1 melee (1d4 / 20)
Sling +4 Ranged (1d3 / 20)
Dagger +1 Melee (1d3 / 19-20)

SPECIAL

Fearless, Keen Senses, Sure footed, Luck, Sneak Attack

FEATS

Alertness

EQUIPMENT

Short Sword (Legacy), Walking Staff, Cloak, Pouch (9), Glass Marble, Quartz Crystal, Dagger (2), Sling

---

XYLA

Elfling   LVL 3
Rogue
HP: 21
AC: 15
Init: +2
base attack: +2
CMB/CMD: +1,+13
Speed: 20

ABILITIES

Str 10
Dex 15
Con 10
Int 11
Wis 9
Cha 16

SAVES

Fort: +2, Ref: +6, Will +1

OFFENSE

Short Sword of Xandra +4 Melee (1d4 / 19-20)
Quarterstaff +3 melee (1d4 / 20)
Sling +5 Ranged (1d3 / 20)
Dagger +3 Melee (1d3 / 19-20)

SPECIAL

Fearless, Keen Senses, Sure footed, Luck, Sneak Attack

FEATS

Alertness, Childlike

EQUIPMENT

Short Sword (Legacy), Walking Staff, Cloak, Pouch (9), Glass Marble, Quartz Crystal, Dagger (2), Sling

TORMAS

HUMAN   **LVL 2**
FIGHTER
HP: 19
AC: 17
INIT: +0
BASE ATTACK: +2
CMB/CMD: +4,+14
SPEED: 20

ABILITIES

STR	15
DEX	11
CON	16
INT	12
WIS	12
CHA	10

SAVES

FORT: +6, REF: +0, WILL +1

OFFENSE

BASTARD SWORD +6 MELEE 2H (1D10+2 / 19-20)
DAGGER +5 MELEE (1D4+2 / 19-20)
DAGGER +3 RANGED (1D4+2 / 19-20)

SPECIAL

SKILLED

FEATS

POWER ATTACK, QUICK DRAW, WEAPON FOCUS, EXOTIC WEAPON

EQUIPMENT

BASTARD SWORD, SCALE ARMOR (LEGACY), BACKPACK, SHORT BOW,

TORMAS

HUMAN   **LVL 3**
FIGHTER
HP: 27
AC: 18
INIT: +0
BASE ATTACK: +3
CMB/CMD: +5,+15
SPEED: 30

ABILITIES

STR	15
DEX	11
CON	16
INT	12
WIS	12
CHA	10

SAVES

FORT: +6, REF: +1, WILL +2

OFFENSE

BASTARD SWORD +6 MELEE 2H (1D10+2 / 19-20)
DAGGER +5 MELEE (1D4+2 / 19-20)
DAGGER +3 RANGED (1D4+2 / 19-20)

SPECIAL

SKILLED

FEATS

POWER ATTACK, QUICK DRAW, WEAPON FOCUS, SHIELD FOCUS, EXOTIC WEAPON

EQUIPMENT

BASTARD SWORD, SCALE ARMOR (LEGACY), BACKPACK, SHORT BOW,

JORISH

Human — LVL 2
Wylder (Mage)
HP: 11
AC: 11
Init: +1
base attack: +1
CMB/CMD: +1,+12
Speed: 30

Abilities

Str	10
Dex	12
Con	9
Int	16
Wis	12
Cha	13

Saves

Fort: -1 Ref: +3 Will +4

Offense

Quarterstaff +1 Melee (1d6 / 20)
Elven Dagger +2 Melee (1d4+1 / 19-20)
Dagger +2 Ranged (1d4+1 / 19-20)
Mana: 5

Special

Spell Sight

Feats

Alertness, Lightning Reflexes, Magical Aptitude

Spells

Lvl 0: Arcane Mark, Dancing Lights

Lvl 1 (1 Mana): Cure Light Wounds, Magic Missle

Equipment

Elven Dagger, Dagger, Walking Staff (Legacy), pouches

JORISH

Human — LVL 3
Wylder (Mage)
HP: 20
AC: 11
Init: +1
base attack: +1
CMB/CMD: +1,+12
Speed: 30

Abilities

Str	10
Dex	12
Con	9
Int	16
Wis	12
Cha	13

Saves

Fort: 0 Ref: +4 Will +4

Offense

Quarterstaff +1 Melee (1d6 / 20)
Elven Dagger +2 Melee (1d4+1 / 19-20)
Dagger +2 Ranged (1d4+1 / 19-20)
Mana: 11

Special

Spell Sight

Feats

Alertness, Lightning Reflexes, Magical Aptitude

Spells

Lvl 0: Arcane Mark, Dancing Lights

Lvl 1 (1 Mana): Cure Light Wounds, Magic Missle

Lvl 2 (3 Mana): Flaming Sphere

Equipment

Elven Dagger, Dagger, Walking Staff (Legacy), pouches

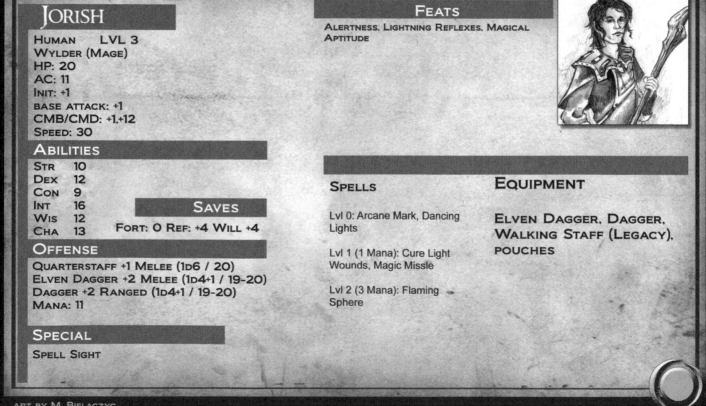

AGNAR

HUMAN   LVL 2
BARBARIAN
HP: 27
AC: 15
INIT: +1
BASE ATTACK: +2
CMB/CMD: +6,+17
SPEED: 30

ABILITIES

STR	18
DEX	12
CON	14
INT	13
WIS	10
CHA	11

SAVES
FORT: +5, REF: +1, WILL +0

OFFENSE

GREATSWORD +6 MELEE (2D6+6 / 19-20)
DAGGER +6 MELEE (1D4+4 /19-20)
DAGGER +3 RANGED (1D4+4 /19-20)

SPECIAL

RAGE

FEATS
CLEAVE, POWER ATTACK

EQUIPMENT

GREATSWORD (LEGACY), HIDE ARMOR, ROPE, CLOAK, BACKPACK

ART BY M. BIELACZYC

AGNAR

HUMAN   LVL 3
BARBARIAN
HP: 35
AC: 15
INIT: +1
BASE ATTACK: +3
CMB/CMD: +7,+18
SPEED: 30

ABILITIES

STR	18
DEX	12
CON	14
INT	13
WIS	10
CHA	11

SAVES
FORT: +5, REF: +2, WILL +1

OFFENSE

GREATSWORD +7 MELEE (2D6+6 / 19-20)
DAGGER +7 MELEE (1D4+4 /19-20)
DAGGER +4 RANGED (1D4+4 /19-20)

SPECIAL

RAGE

FEATS
CLEAVE, POWER ATTACK, IMPROVED BULL RUSH

EQUIPMENT

GREATSWORD (LEGACY), HIDE ARMOR, ROPE, CLOAK, BACKPACK

ART BY M. BIELACZYC

NASIR

HUMAN   **LVL 2**
FIGHTER
HP: 15
AC: 16
INIT: +3
BASE ATTACK: +2
CMB/CMD: +3,+13
SPEED: 30

ABILITIES

STR	13
DEX	17
CON	13
INT	11
WIS	9
CHA	12

SAVES

FORT: +4, REF: +3, WILL -1

OFFENSE

(P) SHORT SWORD +4 MELEE (1D6+1 / 19-20)
(OH) SHORT SWORD +4 MELEE (1D6 / 19-20)
SHORTBOW +5 (1D6 / 20)
DAGGER +3 MELEE (1D4+1 / 19-20)

SPECIAL

ARMOR TRAINING, BRAVERY

FEATS

TWO WEAPON DEFENSE, TWO WEAPON FIGHTING, WEAPON FINESSE, WEAPON FOCUS

EQUIPMENT

SHORT SWORD (LEGACY), SHORT SWORD, SHORTBOW, DAGGER (5)

ART BY SAM FLEGAL

NASIR

HUMAN   **LVL 3**
FIGHTER
HP: 26
AC: 16
INIT: +3
BASE ATTACK: +3
CMB/CMD: +4,+17
SPEED: 30

ABILITIES

STR	13
DEX	17
CON	13
INT	11
WIS	9
CHA	12

SAVES

FORT: +4, REF: +4, WILL +0

OFFENSE

(P) SHORT SWORD +5 MELEE (1D6+1 / 19-20)
(OH) SHORT SWORD +5 MELEE (1D6 / 19-20)
SHORTBOW +6 (1D6 / 20)
DAGGER +4 MELEE (1D4+1 / 19-20)

SPECIAL

ARMOR TRAINING, BRAVERY

FEATS

QUICK DRAW, TWO WEAPON DEFENSE, TWO WEAPON FIGHTING, WEAPON FINESSE, WEAPON FOCUS

EQUIPMENT

SHORT SWORD (LEGACY), SHORT SWORD, SHORTBOW, DAGGER (5)

ART BY SAM FLEGAL

INOLA

WILDE ELF   LVL 2
DRUID LUMINAR
HP: 11
AC: 14
INIT: +2
BASE ATTACK: +1
CMB/CMD: +1,+13
SPEED: 30

ABILITIES

STR   10
DEX   15
CON   9
INT   14
WIS   15
CHA   12

SAVES

FORT: +2, REF: +2, WILL +5

OFFENSE

QUARTERSTAFF +1 (1D6 / 20)
SHORTBOW +3 (1D6 / 20)
DAGGER +1 MELEE (1D4+/ 19-20)

MANA: 5

SPECIAL

ELVEN IMMUNITIES, TRACKLESS STEP,
WILD EMPATHY, WOODLAND STRIDE

FEATS

EMPOWER SPELL

SPELLS

Lvl 0: Dancing Lights,
Detect Poison, Guidance

Lvl 1 (1 Mana): Bless,
Entangle, Magic Weapon

EQUIPMENT

SHORTBOW (LEGACY), DAGGER,
WALKING STAFF, LEATHER
ARMOR, CLOAK, BACKPACK,
POUCHES

ART BY M. BIELACZYC

INOLA

WILDE ELF   LVL 3
DRUID LUMINAR
HP: 15
AC: 14
INIT: +2
BASE ATTACK: +2
CMB/CMD: +2,+14
SPEED: 30

ABILITIES

STR   10
DEX   15
CON   9
INT   14
WIS   15
CHA   12

SAVES

FORT: +2, REF: +3, WILL +5

OFFENSE

QUARTERSTAFF +2 (1D6 / 20)
SHORTBOW +4 (1D6 / 20)
DAGGER +2 MELEE (1D4+/ 19-20)

MANA: 11

SPECIAL

ELVEN IMMUNITIES, TRACKLESS STEP,
WILD EMPATHY, WOODLAND STRIDE

FEATS

COMBAT CASTING, EMPOWER SPELL

SPELLS

Lvl 0: Dancing Lights,
Detect Poison, Guidance

Lvl 1 (1 Mana): Bless,
Entangle, Magic Weapon

Lvl 2 (3 Mana): Cat's
Grace

EQUIPMENT

SHORTBOW (LEGACY), DAGGER,
WALKING STAFF, LEATHER
ARMOR, CLOAK, BACKPACK,
POUCHES

ART BY M. BIELACZYC

GLOSSARY OF PEOPLE AND PLACES

Andros, Malynn	See Malynn.
Anva Babicova	Youngest daughter of Rosada, the nice one who will help the party.
Babicova, Anva	See Anva.
Babicova, Rosaga	See Rosaga.
Babicova, Olesya	See Olesya.
Bechim Todaren	Son of Grigore, play writer, thinks he should be ringmaster.
Belial Fue'vuer	Envoy from Jaeldor who has been training Resly in ravaging magic.
Cameron Todaren	Ringmaster of the circus, passed down from his uncle Grigore.
Conall Babicova	Deceased husband of Rosaga, known as the Two-Faced Man, he was the dominant side of a conjoined twin.
Davin Todaren	Son of Grigore, black sheep, gambler, fortune reader, animal feeder.
Drake	The Dragonman.
Farr, Jirrim	See Jirrim.
Ferryport	The largest city in this region of Uteria.
Fitz	A young street thief, at the circus looking for marks.
Gershak	The Boggart Chief.
Gertras	Sells herbs in a shop in Ferryport.
Garamond	Guard in Ferryport who Silas Monta sometimes contacts to procure services, the adventures have Garamond's trust and have performed several small services for him recently.
Grigore Todaren	Circus owner, uncle of Cameron, father of Bechim and Davin.
Hafsha	A mercenary visiting the circus, looking for trouble.
Jaeldor	The city that Belial Fue'vuer is a visiting oficial from. It is called the Gem of the West, and the capital of the Kingdom of Jaeldor.
Jirrim Farr	Strong man.
Kaia	The sword swallower.
Kaldrath	Viewed by some as a god, he was banished long ago by the Elves, though he lives between worlds.

Kier	Brother of Conall, who existed only as a malformed face on the left side of his brother's head.
Lady Resly	Deceased wife of Lord Resly whom he thinks he has brought back to life, but who is actually inhabited by a Sirin from the Navirim.
Lord Glycyn	Former ruler of Ferryport who was accused of treason and imprisoned. Resly backs him.
Lord Resly	Taris Resly, the villain, philanderer, murdered his wife, tried to bring her back.
Lorthain Tamen	Malynn's traveling companion and protector.
Margo the Magnificent	Margo Eelen, Acrobat, Contortionist, Costumer.
Malynn Andros	From the tower, investigates magic use.
Navirim, the	The Navirim is an otherworldly place, sometimes called the dream world, that is a source for magic and many of the dark creatures that now invade Uteria, also called the Never by the common folk.
Never, the	The common name for the Navirim.
Northbow, Tain	See Tain.
Olesya Babicova	Eldest daughter of Rosaga, evil, will try to stop the party.
Resly	See Lord Resly.
Rosaga Babicova	Seer, summoned entity from the Never, mother of Olesya and Anva.
Silas Monta	Guildmaster of the Agriculture Guild, the lead architect of the democracy of Ferryport, asked Garamond and/or Tain to find an outside party to clear his name.
Todaren	Family name of circus owners.
Tamen, Lorthain	See Lorthain.
Taris Resly	See Lord Resly.
Tain Northbow	Druid who hires the party to clear his friend Silas Monta's name.
Tyr	A city far to the East, that Malynn claims to hail from.
Uteria	The world in which these adventures take place.
Zenia	Bearded mistress of beasts (beast tamer).

THE TOME
OF THE ARTS

A Guide to Magic in Uteria

THE TOME OF THE ARTS

The one rule of magic that is constant is that energy must come from somewhere; it doesn't just appear.

Master Irphazan, Druid Council

I was fifteen when the world changed. I learned at that young age that I was different.

I was a farmer's son, just like most who grew up in the lands around Kowal. I was the same as many, string thin, but taut as a whip from working the fields. I spent my days with my father, learning the trade. My mother and sister had dinner ready for us when we got home. We owned one book, The Tales of Aradan. *My father would read to us each night. That was my only glimpse into a larger world. A book that told of a time of great kingdoms, noble men, and wicked sorcerers.*

Then at fifteen, it all changed.

He was another boy, a few years older than me. He was always a little bit different. He didn't talk to the rest of us. He hated the work in the fields. He burned easily under the sun and his dark hair framed a face that often looked as if he had tasted something sour. And that was the look on his face when I saw him that night. The buildings in the village were on fire. It was Mordreen and all were gathered for the festivities when we first smelled the smoke. It started at the tavern, the place where Isdril's father spent most of his time. I am sure that is what the townsfolk pointed to as the cause of Isdril's break. Maybe it was. But after that night, I was not around to hear the gossip and the blame throwing.

I was wearing a mask to make me look like a dragon when I saw the flickering light from the center of town. I felt drawn to it, though at the time I did not know why. I dropped my bag of sweet cakes and ran.

I found him there, his eyes seeming to glow in the bright fire from the buildings surrounding him. I saw his father's body, as well as a couple others, littered about him. They looked like skeletons, but I would recognize his father's unkempt beard anywhere in the village. He turned to me, his eyes empty of recognition and he raised his hands. I am not sure what happened next. I saw flames arc out from his hands towards me, but lifting my arms, somehow they did not touch me. I rushed him, my only thought to make the fire stop and I grabbed him on either side of his head. I felt something flow through me, it burned my blood and made my heart feel as if it would explode. Then it stopped. Isdril fell limp from my hands, and those who had approached looked at me in fear and shock. I turned and ran. I left my family, my home, and friends behind. Was I touched by the Fey as well?

I spent months wandering the roads, hiding in the dirt and brambles, until I heard of Eredar. A place of magic, but it seemed to call to me. But not the wizards. It was the Archeons, those who stopped magic. Those who made sure that people like Isdril could not hurt others. I found my way there, and I was taken to the Tower of the Guardian.

My small village may sit there unaware, but I am aware, I am the watcher. I am the one who stops those who broke the world.

Aldulf Toorchek, Archeon and Witch Hunter

Excerpts from various teachings, writing, or lectures on magic:

Magic has been part of the world of Uteria ever since there were beings to write or tell history. The song of magic is the beginning and the end of the world.

In the far past, in the god wars, there were awful battles between the two pantheons. Back then, the gods summoned, kidnapped, or conscripted creatures and peoples from all over the heavens, and beyond, to fight in their wars.

But we were born here, and we inherited the wars. The first of Uteria to know what it was to be aware, and we awoke into war. We have no tomes from then, all was lost in the Long Sleep, when the gods froze many of us in a deep sleep that lasted eons. I guess some of them thought it would be a waste to lose all of a race of unique creatures, as they saw us as little more than playthings.

The Elves were there, and the Eldar. They commanded magics almost as awful as the gods themselves. The stories of the slaughter at the hands of those pointy-eared devils makes my spine shudder, even now when those memories have almost faded to dust.

When we awoke, there was a new power in the world. Humans. While the gods destroyed everything with magic, humans just destroyed everything with their inner nature. Sure, sometimes they build giant temples and mounds that can stand the test of time, but mostly they are in a rush. A rush to expand, a rush to build, a rush to build something else a little bigger. And they multiply, like rabbits who overeat and overdrink.

Add on top of that, their ability at weaving the song for destruction is almost as devastating as the gods. In the Great War, magics were used that rivaled what the gods did to this world.

Magic is the power of Uteria, but will also be its destruction.

And that's why I stay here, making my toys, and letting the other younger dwarves head out into that strange world to make their fortunes.

Biggs Nibeng, toy crafter,
Guild of Builders, Greyhelm

Some say the world was barren before the gods came. The Elves believe it was the gods who came down and brought life to the world, singing a song taught to them by the creator and drawing creatures and animals from throughout the heavens to come to Uteria. But I believe that the Creator infused everything with song, so that magic courses through all of creation.

Of course, none of this can be proven. For the past 700 years we have said that the elves had been little more than our imagination and that magic was a divine gift lost to the world. Now it has blessed us again.

I believe that we had just turned a deaf ear to the song of the Creator. We had lost our faith in the dark times, and now that we have shown him our devotion, we have been blessed with miracles once again. Miracles and tests. Not all those who find their way to his song use their power for good. Some are tempted by the dark forces that forever tempt men. They use their power for personal gain, to harm some and elevate others.

This is why we must be diligent in our own faith, and root out those who would cause evil to fall upon our world.

Archbishop Leon of the
Unelesia Church of Sea Haven

Magic has the Foci; Earth, Water, Air, Fire, and Spirit, and the sources; the Self, the World, and the Navirim. Magic is not an external force, it is a link between all these things. We are all connected, and magic binds us. It has no morals, no agenda, it is just the link. What we do with the link defines us as a being.

Teldior Adrastai,
Druid of the Bordon Grove

There is no magic.

Varleen, Wilde Elf Shaman

THE HISTORY OF MAGIC

The history of magic has been greatly disputed throughout the human ages. Since I cannot speak of the experiences of the elves or elflings, the dwarves or the gods, I can only attest to my own studies of magic in the human realms. Our records show that the Druid Council was formed over 2000 years ago. It existed before that as small groups, but we formed our first Grove deep inside the Mysthorn forest. Other groups formed later. The Wizards of Ish formed when that empire rose to power around a thousand years after the Druid Council formed. The Mages of the West formed in 4699 CE. Before the Mages of the West, many of those gifted would spend their days locked away in small cottages on the edges of the wilderness experimenting and testing their powers.

Then there was Uthgard and the Necromancers. Olaekin Baleband, popularly known as the Warlock King, was obsessed with extending his own life. He brought his kingdom to power and his people prospered, but he used that power to subjugate those who opposed him. He gathered some of the best minds and most gifted magic wielders under his care. He believed that the greatest weakness of the powerful was death. His Necromancers found ways to extend his life ten times longer than a normal human's lifespan. During his war against the Aradan Kingdom, his top Necromancers formed the Nulthari, who were the ones who used unspeakable magics to destroy the Eastlands.

And then the War stopped. Magic disappeared in a flicker. Those races most in touch with the power also disappeared. Many theories have tried to explain the Disappearance, but none have proven completely true. The old groups fell apart. The Druid Council fell from grace as people began to mistrust those who once used magic. The Council fell apart and most of our knowledge lost over the centuries. The Mages disbanded when Eredar was destroyed during the Great War, and only reformed a mere 80 years ago.

We are in a time of rebirth when it comes to the Arts. The old groups hold power again. We will see how the new cycles turn now that magic is once again in Uteria.

Aledyn, Druid of Bordon
Traveler of the East

The old lands of the Aradan Kingdom to the east are uninhabitable wasteland. A twisted land that stretches around the old northern Kingdom of Uthgard to the deep south. Magic has been abused throughout our history, and I am here to make sure it does not happen again.

Grand Lord Archeon Techaan
sitting upon the Warden's Throne in
the Tower of the Guardian

Illustration by Michael Bielaczyc

GROUPS OF MAGIC USERS

THE MAGES OF THE TOWER
Formal name: Otari
Other names: Wizards, Warlocks, Sorcerers

The Mages of the Tower are, by far, the most well known in the lands, or at least they are the ones that fill the stories. White haired old men with beards calling down lightning, throwing balls of fire, and causing the walls of the great castles to crumble. The wizards spent their time researching and classifying magic; they felt that magic could be defined and quantified. Their ability to warp energy was beyond any of the other magical groups of Uteria, and that power led to corruption. During the Great War, some wizards left to fight with Uthgard and the armies of the North, becoming the Nulthari. Others aligned themselves with the Aradan Kingdom in the South. Some stayed neutral. This infighting caused the fall and destruction of the Tower, all factions wanting control of the knowledge there.

A hundred years ago, a small group came back to the ruins of the Tower and began to rebuild. Though there was no magic to harness, they taught of the world and its ways. They pushed science and discovery, but often hit dead ends as they could not find common threads between different theories. One day a chemical substance would cause an explosion, and the next day it would not. They surmised that there was some force that altered the state of physics in Uteria.

During the Great War, magic twisted and destroyed the lands in the East, so when the Tower was rebuilt, both the people who studied there and the local governments built a separate tower for the Archeons, or Watchers. They were there to keep watch over the wizards and their power, so that no one could ever harness the great power that laid waste to the lands of the southeast.

Since magic has started to return, the Mages have begun to scour the lands for potential apprentices. At the same time, the Archeons are on the hunt for those who abuse the power of magic.

EREDAR
The Tower of the Mages

Eredar, also called the Tower, is nestled in a mountain range in the middle of the Eastlands. Outside of the mountains is Olsztyn, the closest

Illustration by Paul Bielaczyc

neighboring town. The pass between the two is guarded by the Tower of the Guardian. All are encircled by the Stonewall, a tall stone barrier created by the Mages thousands of years ago.

Olsztyn is divided, old town and new town. Old Town is mostly abandoned. The Melted Keep sits atop its odd steep hill, melted from the magics used in the Great War. New Town is thriving, especially with the commerce between Eredar and themselves.

73

THE DRUIDS

The ancient Druids were formed from tribal magic users who found themselves drawn to the forests, deserts, and other natural places of Uteria. They were heavily influenced by the Elves, seeing magic as part of everything around, a fabric of the world that extended beyond the self and into the stars. Still, following the tendency of humans, they tried to define it, finding the five elements of magic — fire, water, air, earth, and spirit. They also defined the three sources — self, world, and spirit. This differed from the view of magic of the Elves which, simply put, is there is no magic, there is life.

As the Druids progressed, they formed larger communities, knit by a want to make the world a better place. They became the advisors to kings, the lorekeepers, and observers. They built Groves, or places of meeting and meditation, a direct influence from the Elves. These Groves were found inside or around all major cities. In Selardor, the capital of the Aradan Kingdom, the king's castle was built in the center of a Grove itself.

During the Great War, the Druids spent their time defending cities attacked by aggressors, never taking to the offense. Though there was some internal debate to this course of action, it held until the end of the war and the Disappearance.

After the war the Druids lost much of their power, many looking to them as archaic and blasphemous in the time that followed. Those of the Church persecuted them, causing the Groves to fall, and the Druids to become all but extinct.

Seahaven was the one refuge for the Druids. Not as touched by the war as many other places, they were allowed to keep their Grove and tomes in the city proper. As magic has come back into the world, the Druids have begun to expand, finding those who share their views and beliefs to join their ranks. They spent their time rebuilding Groves or searching for old ones, hoping to find some of the vast knowledge lost by war.

THE SHAMANS

The shamans are less an organized group than a type of magic user defined by their part as wise folk and leaders in the wilds and outskirts of the lands.

They know the legends of the lands that surround them and offer those who seek their knowledge freely. They are Wylders by trade, though when tribes meet, some may gain the abilities of a Druidic Luminar.

THE NECROMANCERS

The Necromancers of the Fourth Age live by the codes of the ancient Nulthari of Pardalor. They look to gain power over life, to end suffering and disease, and conquer death. Some see this as an avenue to power; others see this as a way to stop the pain of those suffering.

They also claim to be able to commune with the dead, but many believe that they are only speaking with those of the Navirim or the Between.

The most powerful sect of Necromancers have aligned themselves with the reborn kingdom of Uthgard in the Northeast and taken the name Nulthari once again.

THE UNELESIA CHURCH

There are many churches throughout the lands, but the one most are familiar with is the Unelesia Church, or Church of the One. The Unelesia Church rose in favor after the Great War. The world was suffering, and it gave hope. It told people that with faith and good deeds, your afterlife would be better than life on Uteria. It grew in power and influence swiftly, and became opulent and ritualistic. Then, as the plagues began to ravage the lands, its centralized power weakened and the Church became regional, with each sect having its own set of beliefs.

The Valetta region of the Church saw evil and Kaldrath around all dark corners and persecuted those who they saw as colluding with evil. The Endamas Church was separated from the more strict northern sects and became tolerant and open to the populace.

Now that magic has reemerged, each branch of the Church is struggling to cope with something that complicates their views of faith and spirit.

In the Endamas region of the world, the Unelesia of those regions has welcomed in some of the "blessed." In Ferryport, they have even opened up part of their school to devote to those given the gifts of the Creator.

THE POLYTHESIA

The old religion still holds sway over many regions, and most of the bigger cities host a temple to the old deities. While the Unelesia view the followers of this religion as misguided at best or heretics at worst, the Polythesians are content to their own beliefs and rituals.

They have always had a more open minded view of the world around them and the reemergence of magic only strengthens their beliefs. While the Unelesians see the pantheon of deities as servants of the Creator, the Polythesians see the Creator as an absent father and the deities as the ones who watch over and protect those who ask for their favor.

ARCHEONS – THE WATCHERS

The magic users of Uteria are watched over by the Archeons, or more commonly called the Watchers. After the war against the Warlock King, Olaekin Baleband, the last of the wizards who served the United Kingdoms (Aradan, Norland, and Endamas) formed the Council and began to put forth rules to try and stop the wide use of ruinous magic. They formed the Archeons and trained them in ways to stop magic. Over the 700 years since the end of that war, the Archeons have become quite powerful, not just traveling the lands, but also keeping an eye over all the tower to make sure none begin to use forbidden magic. There are many different factions of Archeons, those who travel the lands hunting Nulthari (The Hunters, called witch hunters by commoners), those who keep an eye over those in Eredar (the Order of the Tower), and those who pair up with an Otari wizard as a guardian and partner (The Keepers).

They have the ability to nullify magic, as well as cut a person off from the energies around them. This takes a great amount of power, and often it takes many Archeons to take down a powerful Nulthari, and even more to permanently pacify a Nulthari.

WIZARDS OF ISH

The Wizards of Ish keep their secrets close. Once trained they are never allowed to leave the ranks of the Sorcerers. Of all the magic groups, theirs was the most untouched during the Disappearance and their stronghold in the center of Ish remains as it has for over a thousand years. But whatever knowledge they may have, they keep to themselves.

Much like the rest of the Ishian Empire, their policies are strict, and death or slavery is a just punishment.

One of the biggest differences between the Wizards of Ish and the majority of other magic using groups is their use of slaves as power reservoirs for magic. Powerful wizards can have a stable of slaves, blank eyed and pale, who are kept on leashes as a source of power for their magic.

THE REBELLION
Mages who fight against the tyranny of the Empire and the Wizards of Ish

The Rebellion is a rather new group of mages who oppose the rule of the Emperor and the Wizards of Ish. They are hunted mercilessly throughout the Empire, but as magic has reawakened, they have grown in numbers and in power.

Secret is their strongest advantage, so very little is known of them.

THE ELVES AND MAGIC

Magic is just part of the everyday life for most elves. In fact, they claim that there is no such thing as the Art and its power. It is just life to them. Elves seems to have all levels of magic users, from those who are powerful enough to shape stone into a fortress, to those who do little more than speak with birds. Since they have such a natural affinity to magic, each elf has their own choice in the level of power behind their magic.

ELFLINGS AND MAGIC

Elflings have no formal rules or laws, so the idea of an elfling school of magic seems far fetched. There are many who are skilled in the Arts among them, but they are as wild with their magic as they are with their view of the world.

DWARVES AND MAGIC

Some among the dwarves seek the discipline of the Arts, and those who do often find themselves to be part of the Dwarven Church. In current day, some have left the strict society and trained under other organizations, such as the Druids and Wizards in the human societies.

FAUNS AND MAGIC

Fauns are much like the elves, having a natural ability with magic. They tend to be focused on nature, much like their culture, becoming Luminars of the Druidic path.

THE MAGIC OF UTERIA

I grew up misunderstood by my family. When my powers first appeared, they thought I was touched by a demon. Luckily, my family had more distrust for authority than my gifts. I grew up being either shunned by my parents and siblings, or coddled for being "weak". Farm life is not the best for one of a thin build and delicate hands. But I was good at problem solving, and my father never turned down an observation or suggestion for getting a better crop.

But when I turned seventeen, my full power came into being. I knew I could sing to a squirrel with a limp and it would bound off as if its leg had never been hurt. But when I reached seventeen cycles my favorite cat Max was mauled by something from the fields. He limped home, one eye missing and his leg nothing but a mangled stump.

As he lay dying in my arms, my family tried comforting me, but also to make it a lesson about toughening up. I was tired of them looking at me that way, so I laid my hands on Max, closed my eyes, began a soft chant, and moved my hands around his broken body. To the horror of my family, Max awoke, the skin around his missing eye healed, leaving a blank white scar, and his leg was no longer mangled, though he still has a limp to this day.

The look on all of their faces told me that it was time to leave. It was time to find my own way in this world, and not look at my gifts as a curse, but instead as a path to making something of myself.

Jorish, explaining his discovery of magic to Malynn, Mage of the Tower

MAGIC IN UTERIA

Magic is a rare gift in Uteria. To account for its unique nature, spellcasting is treated differently than in the base Pathfinder Roleplaying Game system. The system has two distinct differences. First, it is designed to make casting more open and accessible, making spell choice easier and making Metamagic feats more open. Second, it is meant to emphasize the dangerous nature of magic, and why it should be respected and feared in Uteria.

Mages in Uteria are able to cast spells due to mana, a mix between personal energy, the energy from the environment around the caster, and energy from the Navirim, the dream world. They have a limited amount of mana per day, though by ravaging or focusing, a mage may be able to cast more spells than their mana pool normally allows.

MANA POOL

Mana per day

After 8 hours of rest, a spellcaster gains a base mana pool to pull from in order to cast spells. This provides casters with more freedom when picking how they cast spells each day than the standard method. This mana is based on two factors: (1) the character's caster level and (2) their primary spellcasting ability score.

The following table indicates the base mana gained each day (after 8 hours of rest) based on the caster's level.

Table 1: Base Mana per Day	
Caster Level	Mana per Day
1st	2
2nd	4
3rd	7
4th	11
5th	16
6th	24
7th	33
8th	44

Spellcasters can also receive bonus mana if their primary Spellcasting Ability Score is high enough. At first level, a player chooses their spellcaster's primary ability, which all their bonuses are based upon. They can not alter this choice, unless they change a spellcasting class, such as changing from Wylder to Luminar, or Wylder to Fighter.

Most spellcasters in Uteria use Intelligence as their primary spellcasting ability; however, the Story Guide should feel free to allow the use of Wisdom or Charisma for the primary spellcasting ability if it makes for a better story or character development.

To determine your mana bonus, simply consult Table 2 and find the intersection of the row for your primary spellcasting ability score and the column for the maximum spell level your character is capable of casting.

Table 2: Mana Bonus (Based on Spellcasting Ability Score vs. Spellcaster Level)				
Spellcasting Base Ability Score	Level of Spellcaster			
	1-2	3-4	5-6	7-8
12-13	1	1	1	1
14-15	1	4	4	4
16-17	1	4	9	9
18-19	1	4	9	16
20-21	2	5	10	17
22-23	2	8	13	20

To calculate your total mana allowed per day, referred to as your mana pool, just add your base mana to your mana bonus.

MANA POOL = BASE MANA + MANA BONUS

For example, a 5th level luminar with an intelligence of 17 would gain 9 extra mana points per day to add to her base mana of 16, for a total of 25 mana per day (assuming her base ability is intelligence).

PREPARING SPELLS

A spellcaster can cast any spell that they know. They do not have to memorize or pray to gain access to the spell. If the spell is on their known spells list, they are allowed to cast it, as long as they have the mana to do so. The level of spell the caster can cast is still defined by the Core Rules.

LEARNING NEW SPELLS

Since magic has been gone for so long, much of the knowledge and lore of spell casting has been lost as well. While being part of a magic group such as the Otari gives a better chance of expanding your spell knowledge, most spells are learned from ancient scrolls, or directly from other casters. One of the most common ways to learn is through Spell Sight, which is detailed later in this section.

REGAINING MANA

Mana is the source of a spellcaster's essence. As their mana is consumed, it puts a strain on a spellcasters' mind and body. Even though this may not manifest as actual damage or a condition affecting your character, try to think about this when roleplaying your character to add a layer of story to your gaming session.

A spellcaster regains their full mana pool (base mana and bonus mana) after a full 8 hours of rest.

CASTING SPELLS

Each spell has a specific minimum or Basic Mana Cost. More powerful spells cost more mana to cast than weaker ones. Spells are cast at their minimum or basic mana cost, save for one exception: spells that deal damage based on a number of dice (magic missile, searing light, etc.). Rolled damage spells only deal damage as if they were cast at their basic mana cost, unless the caster opts to spend more mana to increase the damage.

Table 3: Basic Mana Cost of Spells by Spell Level	
Spell Level	Base Mana Cost
0	0
1	1
2	3
3	5
4	7

A spellcaster can choose to increase the dice damage of a spell at the time of casting, as long as they don't exceed the maximum mana cost they are able to cast, or the maximum level allowed by the spell. Each additional mana point spent, increases the effective caster level of the spell by 1 level, but only for the purpose of damage dealt by dice.

This is to balance out the "costs" of spells in this variant. Otherwise lower mana spells such as fireball and lightning bolt can grow to become more powerful than higher cost spells, while costing only half as much mana to cast! All other aspects of spells, such as range and duration, are based on the spellcaster's normal caster level.

Example: Astrid is 7th level. She casts fireball, a 3rd level spell. She can either cast it at the basic cost of 5 mana (as if she were 5th level), doing 5d6 damage; or she can choose at the time of casting to put more mana into the spell. Since she is 7th level, she can put up to 7 mana into her fireball. She choses to just add one level to the casting, costing a total of 6 mana. She gets to roll 6d6 for damage because it is as if she were casting it at 6th level, but her range is still based on her class caster level (CL), which is 7th. (Note: this does not affect the spell saving throw DC because that is based on the actual level of the particular spell being cast, not the effective level it was cast at.)

METAMAGIC FEATS AND MANA

Metamagic feats become more versatile in this variant, as they can be determined based on the encounter or predicament that the characters currently face. When casting a spell using a metamagic feat, it uses up mana as if it were cast at a higher level. However, a spellcaster is still limited by the maximum spell cost they can cast. If the metamagic feat would increase the spell beyond what they could normally cast, the spellcaster can't cast the spell using that metamagic feat.

The spell's caster level, in regards to the damage dealt by dice, still follows the rules listed above, using dice based on the basic casting level for the spell. The spellcaster however can choose to spend additional points to increase the effective caster level for damage dealing purposes.

FOCUSING AND RAVAGING

Once a character has exhausted her mana for the day, she must rest for 8 hours to regain it. However, if the need is more desperate, a mage can actually pull energy from the world around her to continue casting, despite the lack of mana. If a spellcaster wants to pull energy directly from herself, she must Focus on her own life essence. Focusing requires concentrated effort to ensure that they only use energy from within themselves, and not accidentally draw the life force from those around them, including creatures, persons, plants, and essentially anything living.

However, converting life energy in this manner is extremely dangerous, and can cause great harm to the spellcaster. When casting a spell without sufficient mana, a spellcaster must make a Concentration check (DC 15 + spell cost). If she fails this check, she takes Mental Fatigue damage equal to the spell's mana cost. If she succeeds, she only takes half damage. On a roll of 1 the spellcaster accidentally ravages.

Mental Fatigue damage can be treated similar to non-lethal damage. It is not deducted from your current hit points, but a running total is kept. If at any point your Mental Fatigue exceeds your current hit points, you fall unconscious. Also, as long as a character has at least one point of Mental Fatigue, he is considered fatigued.

Mental Fatigue is also unique to other forms of damage; it cannot be healed using Cure spells. It only regenerates with time. After a full 8 hours of rest, all Mental Fatigue is healed and all mana is recovered.

Ravagers, on the other hand, do not concern themselves with where the energy comes from. Once they exhaust their spell points, they can continue casting by drawing on the life force of all living matter around them. They have no need to concentrate on where the energy originates from, and no concern for what is harmed by their selfish acts. When casting spells in this manner, all living creatures within a radius of the spellcaster take physical damage. At the Ravager's discretion, one of the following occurs: (1) All living creatures within a 10 foot radius take damage equal to the spell's mana cost, or (2) All creatures take 1 damage in a radius equal to 10 feet times the spell's cost.

Illustration by Michael Bielaczyc

A Ravager's act is instantly recognizable. Anyone within the circle feels their life essence drain from them, usually accompanied by a headache and chills. Even those outside of the affected radius are instantly aware. Small plants, such as grass and weeds, shrivel and turn black. Nearby surfaces of inhabited waters become speckled with small dead fish. Insects become desiccated instantly, like a cicada's molted skin.

Ravaging is an evil act, even when a caster does it out of desperation, or by accident. If a mage is about to die, but must use magic to save his companions, he must make a tough decision to turn to such a desperate act. Other times a mage might make a careless mistake. If a mage rolls a natural 1 on his Concentration check and has a Spellcraft skill less than 10, he will accidentally ravage his surroundings, despite his best intentions. However, once a mage has trained thoroughly and has a skill of at least 10 in Spellcraft (rank plus ability modifier), he needn't worry about this happening by accident. When a caster Ravages, he rolls a D20. On a natural 1, he fails his casting check and will pull the mana directly from himself, causing physical damage equal to the mana cost of the failed spell.

As Ravagers continue to perform these heinous acts, many experience physical changes to their appearance. The effects are subtle at first, dark bags under the eyes, a lingering cough, dry, chapped lips. But then the become more noticeable, sunken eyes, discolored eyes, dark veins running under the skin. Some scholars claim that tales of hideous twisted crones with greenish skin, long hooked noses, and warts were the result of ravagers who overused their powers. If you choose to play a Ravager, be creative with the effects of the magic, to make the character your own.

RAVAGE POINTS (OPTIONAL)

As a spellcaster Ravages, her appearance can change as well as how others perceive her. As you gain Ravage Points, you become corrupted and your appearance changes. An adventurer can rid herself of Ravage Points by doing things that the Story Guide deems as redemptive.

Ravage Points	Suggested Corruptions
1-2	No appearance change.
3-4	Dark shadows around eyes, bluish lips
5-6	Pale skin, slight showing of veins.
7-8	Hair becomes stringy, or loss of hair.
9-10	Eyes become pale, bloodshot.
11-12	Eyes sink, skin becomes pale or bluish.
13-14	Loss of weight, elongated fingernails. People feel uncomfortable around you.
15-16	Teeth become stained, hair is thin.
17-18	Stooped posture, pale skin becomes wrinkled or glossy.
19	Eyes become all white. Can not hide the aura of evil around you.
20	Hair falls out, skin pulled tight over bones.

SPELLCASTING CLASSES

WYLDERS AND LUMINAR

There are two basic spellcasting classes in Uteria: Wylders and Luminar. Wylders are wild mages, untrained, self taught, and unpredictable. They have a natural talent for the arts, and have led themselves on a path of discovery of the deeper magics. Luminar are the formally trained magic users of Uteria, who have apprenticed under a more powerful luminari. They have different focuses, but their base abilities are all the same.

WYLDER

Untrained in the delicate and precise nature of magic, some wylders have learned through trial and error how to live with their special gifts, while others perished due to the dangerous effects of their gift. Raised in a world that fears magic, wylders strive to keep their abilities a secret and try to live a normal life. Instead of isolating themselves in the intense study of magic like the luminari, they go about their lives, becoming proficient with more weapons and armor, honing their skills, and leading more active lives, granting them more toughness than their learned counterparts. Wylders aren't trained in the intricate symbols and writings used to record spells, so while wylders are able to Read Scrolls and Read Magic, they are unable to scribe their own spells, either on scrolls or in a spellbook.

Hit Die: d8.

CLASS SKILLS

The wylder's class skills are Appraise (Int), Bluff (Cha), Craft (Int), Diplomacy (Cha), Handle Animal (Cha), Heal (Wis), Intimidate (Cha), Perception (Wis), Profession (Wis), Ride (Dex), Sense Motive (Wis), Spellcraft (Int), and Survival (Wis).

Skill Ranks per Level: 4 + Int modifier.

CLASS FEATURES

The following are the class features of the wylder.

Weapon and Armor Proficiency: Wylders are proficient with all simple weapons, light armor, medium armor, and shields (except tower shields). A wylder's movements are impaired by wearing armor and shields, and thus they still suffer a chance of spell failure, but only when casting spells with

Level	Base Attack Bonus	Fort Save	Ref Save	Will Save	Special
1st	+0	+2	+0	+2	Spell Memory, Spell Sight, Cantrips, Read Scroll, Wild Magic
2nd	+1	+3	+0	+3	
3rd	+2	+3	+1	+3	Bonus magical feat, Casting Focus
4th	+3	+4	+1	+4	
5th	+3	+4	+1	+4	
6th	+4	+5	+2	+5	Improved Casting Focus
7th	+5	+5	+2	+5	
8th	+6/+1	+6	+2	+6	Focused Wild Magic

Table 4: Wylder Class Bonuses

somatic components. A wylder can discard her shield according to the Combat rules for dropping a shield to avoid the spell failure chance when casting.

Spells: A wylder casts spells drawn from any of their spells that are currently committed to Spell Memory. This does not include spells which are still being studied and committed to memory.

To learn, prepare, or cast a spell, the wylder must have a chosen base ability score equal to at least 10 + the spell level.

The Difficulty Class for a saving throw against a wylder's spell is 10 + the spell's level + the wylder's ability modifier.

Spell Saving Throw DC = 10 + spell level + spellcasting ability score bonus

A wylder casts spells using mana. Each spell has a certain cost, and as long as she has the mana available, she may cast the spell without incident. However, once a wylder runs out of spell points, she can continue casting spells, but the mana must be pulled either from her own essence or from the environment surrounding her. To ravage the life force from others is considered a vile act, and is only done by those who are evil at heart, or as a desperate act by

Illustration by Mitch Foust

good characters. (Please see the section on Focusing and Ravaging for more.)

The daily base mana pool was defined in Table 1, and is duplicated here for the reader's convenience. In addition this base pool, wylders receive bonus mana each day depending on their Intelligence score (see Table 2: Mana Bonus).

Table 1: Base Mana Per Day

Caster Level	Mana per Day
1st	2
2nd	4
3rd	7
4th	11
5th	16
6th	24
7th	33
8th	44

Table 2: Mana Bonus (Based on Spellcasting Ability Score vs. Spellcaster Level)

Spellcasting Base Ability Score	Level of Spellcaster			
	1-2	3-4	5-6	7-8
12-13	1	1	1	1
14-15	1	4	4	4
16-17	1	4	9	9
18-19	1	4	9	16
20-21	2	5	10	17
22-23	2	8	13	20

Spell Memory: Unable to record spells in a spellbook, wylders are limited to a number of spells they can know at a given time, based on class, level, and ability score. A wylder may have committed to memory a number of spells equal to their *Spell Memory Allotment* for a given spell level plus their primary ability score modifier.

The wylder's default *spell memory allotment* is listed by spellcaster level in Table 5.

For example, Xanthas, a 2nd level wylder, can keep five zero level spells and two 1st level spells in his spell memory by default (Table 5). In addition, he has an intelligence of 17 (and intelligence is his chosen primary ability score). Per the Core Rulebook, his

Table 5: Wylder Spell Memory Allotment by Level

Spellcaster Level	Allowed Spells in Memory by Spell Level				
	0	1st	2nd	3rd	4th
1	4	2	—	—	—
2	5	2	—	—	—
3	5	3	—	—	—
4	6	3	1	—	—
5	6	4	2	—	—
6	7	4	2	1	—
7	7	5	3	2	—
8	8	5	3	2	1

ability modifier for an intelligence score of 17 is +3, so he has the ability to memorize 3 additional spells per spell level above his defaults, that is +3 zero level, +3 1st level, because he is only 2nd level. This gives him the ability to keep a total of eight zero level and five 1st level spells in his spell memory.

A wylder can learn new spells either by reading them from scrolls, or by witnessing another spellcaster in the process of casting the spell. However, she cannot learn new spells from a spellbook, as spellbooks are scribed in a manner that is indecipherable to a wylder.

Spell Sight: A wylder can use Spell Sight to memorize a spell that she witnesses being physically cast (but not a spell cast from a scroll or magical device). To successfully memorize a new spell, a wylders must make a Spellcraft check (DC 18 + the spell's cost) immediately when she sees a spell being cast. If her Spell Sight check is successful and she has an available slot in memory, the spell is learned, but still must be studied before it can be prepared. She has a number of days equal to her primary casting ability bonus to begin committing the spell to Spell Memory, otherwise the intricacies of the spell slip from her mind.

If a wylder has reached her limit for memorizing spells of a specific cost, she can choose to forget any other memorized spell of the same mana cost in order to learn the new spell. However, once forgotten, a spell immediately vanishes from memory, and can not be relearned unless the wylder finds another opportunity to observe that specific spell again. So the wylder must make a split second decision on whether to memorize the new spell or not.

Once a spell is learned, it requires intensive studying to understand the intricacies of the spell.

For a wylder, especially without the formal training in the magical arts, this is a very difficult and time consuming process. To memorize a new spell requires at least 1 hour per day of uninterrupted study/meditation (but no more than 8 hours per day), for a number of hours equal to the spell's cost squared. So a 3-mana spell takes 9 hours of relaxed meditation (minimum of 1 hour per day, not to exceed 8 hours per day), to fully master. Therefore, a 3-mana spell (i.e. a 2nd level spells) would take a minimum of 2 days to learn, whereas a 7-mana spell (i.e. a 4th level spell), would take 49 hours or a minimum of 7 days to learn.

Cantrips: Wylders can prepare a number of cantrips, or 0-level spells, each day, as noted in Table 5: Wylder Spell Memory by Level. These spells are cast like any other spell, but they use no mana when cast and may be cast as often as wanted.

Read Scroll: At 1st level, a wylder has the ability to read magical scrolls, but not spellbooks. Spells found on scrolls can be committed to Spell Memory, but the scroll is lost in the process.

Wild Magic: A burst of energy explodes from your hands towards a target. You must succeed at a ranged touch attack +2. It causes 1d4+1 points of damage, doubling in power every 2 levels. It is a force effect. A wylder can only use this ability 6 times per day.

Casting Focus: As a wylder continues to grow both in the magical and mundane arts, she learns how to maneuver in armor while still maintaining the somatic components of her spells. Upon reaching 3rd level, she can reduce her spell failure chance by 10%.

Improved Casting Focus: Through practice and experience, a wylder has mastered casting spells while wearing armor and carrying a shield. Upon reaching 6th level, she can ignore the failure chance on all light shields, bucklers, and bracers, and reduces her armor spell failure chance by an incredible 20%.

Focused Wild Magic: At level 8, a Wylder has learned to control the wild magics that flow through them. When they turn level 8, their wild magic ability allows them to cast a burst of wild force doing 4d4+4 points of damage, up to 6 times per day. Now that they can focus this energy, they can change the energy type to any in which they choose — acid, fire, force, ice, water, or wind.

LUMINAR
Trained Magic User

Able to draw upon the lifeforce of the world around them, mages are able to work wonders beyond what man thinks possible. While some are able to harness these powers without training, these wylders will never truly appreciate or understand all that can be accomplished with their gift. The true mages of the world have had the opportunity to formally train in the Art of Magic and are known as the Luminari. In a world where magic is rare and seen with suspicion, the Luminari are feared, whether they fight for good, or for evil.

Hit Die: based on training path.

CLASS SKILLS

The luminar's class skills are based on the training path they choose.

Skill Ranks per Level: 2 + Int modifier.

Level	Base Attack Bonus	Fort Save	Ref Save	Will Save	Special
1st	+0	+1	+0	+2	Spell Book, Cantrips, Scribe Scroll, Spell Sight, Bonus magical feat
2nd	+1	+1	+0	+3	
3rd	+1	+2	+1	+3	Bonus magical feat
4th	+2	+2	+1	+4	Circle of Focus
5th	+2	+2	+1	+4	
6th	+3	+3	+2	+5	Bonus magical feat
7th	+3	+3	+2	+5	
8th	+4	+3	+2	+6	Focus Mastery

Table 6: Luminar Class Bonuses

CLASS FEATURES

The following are the class features of the Luminar.

Weapon and Armor Proficiency: Luminari are proficient with the club, dagger, heavy crossbow, light crossbow, and quarterstaff, but not with any type of armor or shield. Armor interferes with a luminar's movements, which can cause his spells with somatic components to fail.

Spells: A luminar casts spells drawn from any of their known spells. This does not include spells which are still being researched and scribed into their books. A luminar may know any number of spells, often being scribed into a spellbook, rune stones, or other archival method.

To learn or cast a spell, the luminar must have a primary ability score equal to at least 10 + the spell level. The Difficulty Class for a saving throw against a luminar's spell is 10 + the spell level + the luminar's spellcasting ability score bonus.

Spell Saving Throw DC = 10 + spell level + spellcasting ability score bonus

A luminar casts spells using mana. Each spell has a certain cost, and as long as he has the mana available, he may cast the spell without incident. However, once a luminar runs out of mana, he can continue casting spells, but at a cost. The mana must be pulled from somewhere, either his own essence, or from the living creatures surrounding him. To ravage the life force from others though is considered a vile act, and is only done by those who are evil at heart, or as a desperate act by good characters. Please see the section on Focusing and Ravaging.

The base mana per day was defined in Table 1, and is duplicated again below for convenience. In addition, luminari receive bonus mana per day depending on their primary spellcasting ability score bonus (see Table 2: Mana Bonus below).

Table 1: Base Mana Per Day

Character Level	Mana per Day
1st	2
2nd	4
3rd	7
4th	11
5th	16
6th	24
7th	33
8th	44

Table 2: Mana Bonus (Based on Ability Score vs. Spellcaster Level)

Base Primary Ability Scoree	Spellcaster's / Luminar's Level			
	1-2	3-4	5-6	7-8
12-13	1	1	1	1
14-15	1	4	4	4
16-17	1	4	9	9
18-19	1	4	9	16
20-21	2	5	10	17
22-23	2	8	13	20

Table 6: Luminar Spells

Luminar Level	Highest Allowed Spell Level
1st	1
2nd	1
3rd	2
4th	2
5th	3
6th	3
7th	4
8th	4

Spell Book: As soon as a Luminar begins his formal training, he is given his own spell book. This book is filled with all the spells that the Luminar has seen and read through his travels, and is considered his most precious treasure in the world. To lose this book is to lose everything that makes him who he is, and potentially gives the finder of the book access to a wealth of spells and knowledge.

Upon first receiving a spellbook, a Luminar's spellbook should contain a number of 0 mana cost spells equal to half his INT score, a number of 1-mana cost spells equal to his primary spellcasting ability bonus, and a number of 3-mana cost spells equal to half his INT modifier (round down for all 3).

All spells are available for a Luminar to learn. They are are only limited by the spell level to record new spells into their spellbook. They can learn new spells by reading other luminari spellbooks (follow the standard rules found in Chapter 9 of the *Pathfinder Roleplaying Game Core Rulebook*), studying them from scrolls, or by witnessing another Luminar in the process of casting a spell from memory, but not casting from a scroll. This last process is called Spell Sight.

Spell Sight: A Luminar can use Spell Sight to memorize a spell that he witnesses being cast from memory, but not a spell cast from a scroll or device. To successfully memorize a new spell, a Luminar must make a Spellcraft check (DC 15 + the spell's level) immediately when he sees a spell being cast. If his Sight is successful, he has number of days equal to his primary ability bonus to begin recording the spell in his spellbook, otherwise the intricacies of the spell slip from his memory.

Learning the intricacies of the spell learned through Spell Sight is not nearly as difficult for a

Luminar when compared to a Wylder. It requires at least 1 hour per day of uninterrupted study/meditation (not to exceed 8 hours in a single day), for a number of hours equal to the spell cost. So a spell costing 5 mana takes 5 hours of relaxed meditation (minimum of 1 hour per day) to fully master.

Cantrips: Luminar can prepare a number of cantrips, or 0-level spells, each day, as noted on Table: Spells per Day. These spells are cast like any other spell, but they are not expended when cast and may be used again.

Scribe Scroll: At 1st level, a luminar gains Scribe Scroll as a bonus feat.

Bonus Feats: At 1st, 3rd, and 6th level, a luminar gains a bonus feat related to being a caster. At each such opportunity, he can choose a metamagic feat, an item creation feat, or Spell Mastery. The luminar must still meet all prerequisites for a bonus feat, including caster level minimums.

These bonus feats are in addition to the feats that a character of any class gets from advancing levels. The luminar is not limited to the categories of item creation feats, metamagic feats, or Spell Mastery when choosing those feats.

TRAINING PATHS OF THE LUMINARI
CIRCLE OF FOCUS

Upon reaching 4th level in any of the following paths, a luminar concludes his training, becoming an equal with the other luminar within his path. By fulfilling his training within his Circle of Focus, he is granted certain special abilities depending on whether he trained within the Mage's Tower, the Druid Council, or the Church.

ADEPT LUMINARI

A luminar trained by the Wizard's Tower or other "arcane" schools receives the following class abilities: Mystic Bond and a bonus Metamagic feat.

A Mystic Bond is formed between the luminar and an object that was a part of his training in the Mage's Tower. Objects that are the subject of this bond must be one of the following: amulet, ring, staff, or weapon. These objects are always masterwork quality. Weapons acquired at 1st level are not made of any special material. If the object is an amulet or ring, it must be worn to have effect, while staves, and weapons must be held in one hand.

Illustration by Mitch Foust

A bonded object can be used once per day to cast any one spell that the luminar has in his spellbook and is capable of casting, even if the spell is not prepared. This spell is treated like any other spell cast by the luminar, including casting time, duration, and other effects dependent on the luminar's level, however it doesn't cost any mana to cast. This spell cannot be modified by metamagic feats or other abilities.

A luminar can add additional magic abilities to his bonded object as if he has the required Item Creation feats and if he meets the level prerequisites of the feat. For example, a luminar with a bonded dagger must be at least 5th level to add magic abilities to the dagger (see Craft Magic Arms and Armor feat). The magic properties of a bonded object, including any magic abilities added to the object, only function for the luminar who owns it. If a bonded object's owner dies, or the item is replaced, the object reverts to being an ordinary masterwork item of the appropriate type.

If a bonded object is damaged, it is restored to full hit points the next time the luminar prepares his spells. If the object of a mystic bond is lost or destroyed, it can be replaced after 1 week in a special ritual that costs 200 gp per luminar level plus the cost of the masterwork item. This ritual takes 8 hours to complete. Items replaced in this way do not possess any of the additional enchantments of the previous bonded item. A luminar can designate an existing magic item as his bonded item. This functions in the same way as replacing a lost or destroyed item except that the new magic item retains its abilities while gaining the benefits and drawbacks of becoming a bonded item.

Upon reaching 6th level, a bonded object can now store 2 different spells, following the rules stated above.

Focus Mastery

Focused Spellmastery — Once per day, you are able to take a spell that you know, and boost its ability by adding mana to its casting cost. Each time you add 2 mana, the spell adds another die to its dice pool.

DRUIDIC LUMINARI

A luminar who studies within the Druid Council for four levels receives the following class abilities immediately at their next level as a full Druid: Natural Armor Proficiency, Nature Sense (Ex), Wild Empathy (Ex), and Woodland Stride (Ex), Trackless Step (Ex) and Animal Companion.

At 6th level, Druidic Luminari gains the ability, Resist Navirim's Lure (Ex), gaining a +4 bonus on saving throws against the spell-like and supernatural abilities of creatures from the Navirim.

Focus Mastery

At 8th level, a Druid receives the Wild Shape Ability.

DEVOUT LUMINARI

A luminar who studies within the church receives the following class abilities immediately at 4th level: Religious Relic and Channel Energy 2d6 (Su). Religious Relic works the same as Arcane Bond, but is an object given by the church to the luminar. This object is a relic of the church, and is as important to the luminar as their spellbook.

A Devout Luminar uses his religious relic as his focus for channeling energy. Upon reaching 5th level, Channel Energy improves to 3d6, and at 6th level improves to 4d6. The relic must be held and lifted to the sky in order to channel energy.

At 6th level, a Devout Luminar gains the ability Heightened Healing. This grants a bonus to all cure spells to heal an additional amount of damage equal to the mana cost of the spell.

Focus Mastery

Channel Energy — At level 8, a devout can channel energy to heal or harm. The devout can take 4d6+4 of energy and use as they wish. Up to three times per day, they may use this energy on targeted creatures within a 30' radius. They can choose to include or exclude themselves in this energy.

LEGACY ITEMS

Certain items gain power as the adventurer levels. These items are a part of the adventurer's story, they are the famed sword, the lockpicks of luck, the rope that their mother gave them before they left home.

These items are part of the legacy of the adventurer.

Other Legacy Items — Other items can be legacy items and it is up to the player and the SG to define the powers of these items.

LEVELING

As an adventurer gains levels, they gain abilities that make their extraordinary. Below is the chart of gained abilities.

Level	Advancement for Weapons
1st	
2nd	Add one more to crit threat 20=19-20; 19-20=18-20
3rd	
4th	+1 to one legacy weapon
5th	
6th	
7th	
8th	+2 to one legacy weapon

Level	Advancement for Armor
1st	
2nd	-1 DR
3rd	
4th	+1 to armor
5th	
6th	
7th	
8th	+2 to armor

Level	Advancement
1st	One Legacy Item
2nd	Bonus Hit Point
3rd	All resistances gain +1
4th	+1 to any ability score, Second Legacy Item
5th	Deflection bonus to AC +1
6th	Resistances gain +1
7th	Natural Armor +1
8th	+2 to any ability score, Third Legacy Item

SPELLS OF UTERIA

0 LEVEL SPELLS

Arcane Mark	Inscribes a personal rune (visible or invisible).
Cure Minor Wounds	Cures 1 point of damage.
Daze	Creature loses next action.
Dancing Lights	Figment torches or other lights.
Detect Magic	Detects spells and magic items within 60 ft.
Detect Poison	Detects poison in one creature or small object.
Disrupt Undead	Deals 1d6 damage to one undead.
Energy Burst	You fire a small orb of energy (caster's focus) at the target. You must succeed on a ranged touch attack to hit your target. The orb deals 1d3 +1 points of chosen energy damage. Energy: Fire, Ice, Acid, Stone, Air.
Flare	Dazzles one creature (-1 attack).
Ghost Sound	Figment sounds.
Guidance	+1 on one roll, throw, or check.
Inflict Minor Wounds	Touch attack, 1 point of damage.
Know Direction	The caster discerns north.
Light	Object shines like a torch.
Mage Hand	5-lb. telekinesis.
Mending	Makes minor repairs on an object.
Open/Close	Opens or closes small or light things.
Purify Food and Drink	Purifies 1 cu. ft./level of food or water.
Prestidigitation	Performs minor tricks.
Read Magic	Read scrolls and spellbooks.
Resistance	Subject gains +1 on saving throws.
Virtue	Subject gains 1 temporary hp.

1ST LEVEL SPELLS

Alarm	Wards an area for 2 hours/level.
Animal Friendship	Gains permanent animal companions.
Animate Rope	Makes a rope move at the caster's command.
Bane	Enemies suffer -1 attack, -1 on saves against fear.
Bless	Allies gain +1 attack and +1 on saves against fear.
Burning Hands	1d4 fire damage/level (max: 5d4).
Calm Animals	Calms 2d4 +1/level HD of animals, beasts, and magical beasts.
Cause Fear	One creature flees for 1d4 rounds.
Change Self	Changes the caster's appearance.
Charm Person	Makes one person the caster's friend.

Chill Touch	1 touch/level deals 1d6 damage and possibly 1 Str damage.
Color Spray	Knocks unconscious, blinds, or stuns 1d6 weak creatures.
Command	One subject obeys one-word command for 1 round.
Comprehend Languages	Understand all spoken and written languages.
Cure Light Wounds	Cures 1d8 +1/level damage (max +5).
Curse Water	Makes unholy water.
Deathwatch	Sees how wounded subjects within 30 ft. are.
Detect Snares and Pits	Reveals natural or primitive traps.
Detect Secret	Doors Reveals hidden doors within 60 ft.
Detect Undead	Reveals undead within 60 ft.
Divine Favor	The caster gains attack, damage bonus, +1/three levels.
Doom	One subject suffers -2 on attacks, damage, saves, and checks.
Endure Elements	Ignores 5 damage/round from one energy type.
Enlarge	Object or creature grows +10%/level (max +50%).
Entangle	Plants entangle everyone in 40-ft.-radius circle.
Entropic Shield	Ranged attacks against the caster suffer 20% miss chance.
Erase	Mundane or magical writing vanishes.
Expeditious	Retreat Doubles the caster's speed.
Faerie Fire	Outlines subjects with light, canceling blur, concealment, etc.
Feather Fall	Objects or creatures fall slowly.
Floating Disk	3-ft.-diameter horizontal disk that holds 100 lb./level.
Goodberry	2d4 berries each cure 1 hp (max 8 hp/24 hours).
Grease	Makes 10-ft. square or one object slippery.
Hold Portal	Holds door shut.
Hypnotism	Fascinates 2d4 HD of creatures.
Identify	Determines single feature of magic item.
Inflict Light Wounds	Touch, 1d8 +1/level damage (max +5).
Invisibility to Animals	Animals can't perceive one subject/leve
Invisibility to Undead	Undead can't perceive one subject/level.
Jump	Subject gets +30 on Jump checks.
Mage Armor	Gives subject +4 armor bonus.
Magical Aura	Grants object false magic aura.
Magic Missile	1d4+1 damage; +1 missile/two levels above 1st (max 5).
Magic Stone	Three stones gain +1 attack, deal 1d6+1 damage.
Magic Weapon	Weapon gains +1 bonus.
Message	Whispered conversation at distance.
Obscuring Mist	Fog surrounds the caster.
Pass without Trace	One subject/level leaves no tracks.
Random Action	One creature acts randomly for one round.
Ray of Enfeeblement	Ray reduces Str by 1d6 points +1 point/two levels.
Reduce	Object or creature shrinks 10%/level (max 50%).

Remove Fear	+4 on saves against fear for one subject +1/four levels.
Sanctuary	Opponents can't attack the caster, and the caster can't attack.
Shield	Invisible disc gives cover and blocks magic missiles.
Shocking Grasp	Touch delivers 1d8 +1/level electricity.
Silent Image	Creates minor illusion of the caster's design.
Sleep	Put 2d4 HD of creatures into comatose slumber.
Spider Climb	Grants ability to walk on walls and ceilings.
Summon Monster I	Calls outsider to fight for the caster.
True Strike	Adds +20 bonus to the caster's next attack roll.
Undetectable Aura	Masks magic item's aura.
Unseen Servant	Creates invisible force that obeys the caster's commands.
Ventriloquism	Throws voice for 1 min./level.

2ND LEVEL SPELLS

Acid Arrow	Ranged touch attack; 2d4 damage for 1 round + 1 round/three levels.
Aid	+1 attack, +1 on saves against fear, 1d8 temporary hit points.
Alter Self	As change self, plus more drastic changes.
Animal Messenger	Sends a Tiny animal to a specific place.
Animal Trance	Fascinates 2d6 HD of animals.
Arcane Lock	Magically locks a portal or chest.
Augury	Learns whether an action will be good or bad.
Barkskin	Grants +3 natural armor bonus (or higher).
Blindness/Deafness	Makes subject blind or deaf.
Blur	Attacks miss subject 20% of the time.
Bull's Strength	Subject gains 1d4+1 Str for 1 hr./level.
Cat's Grace	Subject gains 1d4+1 Dex for 1 hr./level.
Calm Emotions	Calms 1d6 subjects/level, negating emotion effects.
Call Element	Element of Choice is summoned caling 2d6 damage to every creature in radius.
Charm Person or Animal	Makes one person or animal the caster's friend.
Chill Metal	Cold metal damages those who touch it.
Consecrate	Fills area with positive energy, making undead weaker.
Continual Flame	Makes a permanent, heatless torch.
Cure Moderate Wounds	Cures 2d8 +1/level damage (max +10).
Darkness	20-ft. radius of supernatural darkness.
Darkvision	See 60 ft. in total darkness.
Daylight	60-ft. radius of bright light.
Death Knell	Kills dying creature; the caster gain 1d8 temporary hp, +2 Str, and +1 level.
Delay Poison	Stops poison from harming subject for 1 hour/level.
Desecrate	Fills area with negative energy, making undead stronger.

Detect Thoughts	Allows "listening" to surface thoughts.
Endurance	Gain 1d4+1 Con for 1 hr./level.
Enthrall	Captivates all within 100 ft. + 10 ft./level.
Find Traps	Notice traps as a rogue does.
Fire Trap	Opened object deals 1d4 +1/level damage.
Flame Blade	Touch attack deals 1d8 +1/two levels damage.
Flaming Sphere	Rolling ball of fire, 2d6 damage, lasts 1 round/level.
Fog Cloud	Fog obscures vision
Gentle Repose	Preserves one corpse.
Ghoul Touch	Paralyzes one subject, who exudes stench (-2 penalty) nearby.
Glitterdust	Blinds creatures, outlines invisible creatures.
Heat Metal	Hot metal damages those who touch it.
Hideous Laughter	Subject loses actions for 1d3 rounds.
Hold Animal	Holds one animal helpless; 1 round/level.
Hold Person	Holds one person helpless; 1 round/level.
Hypnotic Pattern	Fascinates 2d4+1 HD/level of creatures.
Inflict Moderate Wounds	Touch attack, 2d8 +1/level damage (max +10).
Invisibility	Subject is invisible for 10 min./level or until it attacks.
Knock	Opens locked or magically sealed door.
Lesser Restoration	Dispels magic ability penalty or repairs 1d4 ability damage.
Levitate	Subject moves up and down at the caster's direction.
Locate Object	Senses direction toward object (specific or type).
Magic Mouth	Speaks once when triggered.
Make Whole	Repairs an object.
Minor Image	As silent image, plus some sound.
Mirror Image	Creates decoy duplicates of the caster (1d4 +1/three levels, max 8).
Misdirection	Misleads divinations for one creature or object.
Obscure Object	Masks object against divination.
Produce Flame	1d4 +1/two levels damage, touch or thrown.
Protection from Arrows	Subject immune to most ranged attacks.
Pyrotechnics	Turns fire into blinding light or choking smoke.
Remove Paralysis	Frees one or more creatures from paralysis, hold, or slow.
Resist Elements	Ignores 12 damage/round from one energy type.
Rope Trick	Up to eight creatures hide in extradimensional space.
Scare	Panics creatures up to 5 HD (15-ft. radius).
See Invisibility	Reveals invisible creatures or objects.
Shatter	Sonic vibration damages objects or crystalline creatures.
Shield Other	The caster takes half of subject's damage.
Silence	Negates sound in 15-ft. radius.
Sound Burst	Deals 1d8 sonic damage to subjects; may stun them.
Soften Earth and Stone	Turns stone to clay or dirt to sand or mud.

Speak with Animals	The caster can communicate with natural animals.
Spectral Hand	Creates disembodied glowing hand to deliver touch attacks.
Spiritual Weapon	Magical weapon attacks on its own.
Summon Monster II	Calls outsider to fight for the caster.
Summon Swarm	Summons swarm of small crawling or flying creatures
Trap	Makes item seem trapped.
Tree Shape	The caster looks exactly like a tree for 1 hour/level.
Warp Wood	Bends wood (shaft, handle, door, plank).
Web	Fills 20-ft-radius spread with sticky spider webs.
Whispering Wind	Sends a short message one mile/level.
Wood Shape	Rearranges wooden objects to suit the caster.
Zone of Truth	Subjects within range cannot lie.

3RD LEVEL SPELLS

Animate Dead	Creates undead skeletons and zombies.
Bestow Curse	-6 to an ability; -4 on attacks, saves, and checks; or 50% chance of losing each action.
Blindness/Deafness	Makes subject blind or deaf.
Blink	The caster randomly vanishes and reappears for 1 round/level.
Call Lightning	Directs lightning bolts (1d10/level) during storms.
Clairaudience/Clairvoyance	Hear or see at a distance for 1 min./level.
Contagion	Infects subject with chosen disease.
Continual Flame	Makes a permanent, heatless torch.
Cure Serious Wounds	Cures 3d8 +1/level damage (max +15).
Daylight	60-ft. radius of bright light.
Deeper Darkness	Object sheds absolute darkness in 60-ft. radius.
Diminish Plants	Reduces size or blights growth of normal plants.
Dispel Magic	Cancels magical spells and effects.
Displacement	Attacks miss subject 50%.
Dominate Animal	Subject animal obeys silent mental commands.
Explosive Runes	Deals 6d6 damage when read.
Flame Arrow	Shoots flaming projectiles (extra damage) or fiery bolts (4d6 damage).
Fly	Subject flies at speed of 90.
Fireball	1d6 damage per level, 20-ft. radius.
Gaseous Form	Subject becomes insubstantial and can fly slowly.
Gentle Repose	Preserves one corpse.
Glyph of Warding	Inscription harms those who pass it.
Greater Magic Fang	One natural weapon of subject creature gets +1 bonus to attack and damage per three caster levels (max +5)
Greater Magic Weapon	+1/three levels (max +5).
Gust of Wind	Blows away or knocks down smaller creatures.

Halt Undead	Immobilizes undead for 1 round/level.
Haste	Extra partial action and +4 AC.
Helping Hand	Ghostly hand leads subject to the caster.
Hold Person	Holds one person helpless; 1 round/level.
Illusory Script	Only intended reader can decipher.
Inflict Serious Wounds	Touch attack, 3d8 +1/level damage (max +15).
Invisibility Purge	Dispels invisibility within 5 ft./level.
Invisibility Sphere	Makes everyone within 10 ft. invisible.
Keen Edge	Doubles normal weapon's threat range.
Lightning Bolt	Electricity deals 1d6 damage/level.
Locate Object	Senses direction toward object (specific or type).
Magic Vestment	Armor or shield gains +1 enhancement/three levels.
Major Image	As silent image, plus sound, smell and thermal effects.
Meld into Stone	The caster and the caster's gear merge with stone.
Negative Energy Protection	Subject resists level and ability drains.
Neutralize Poison	Detoxifies venom in or on subject.
Nondetection	Hides subject from divination, scrying.
Obscure Object	Masks object against divination.
Phantom Steed	Magical horse appears for 1 hour/level.
Plant Growth	Grows vegetation, improves crops.
Poison	Touch deals 1d10 Con damage, repeats in 1 min.
Protection from Elements	Absorb 12 damage/level from one kind of energy.
Remove Blindness/Deafness	Cures normal or magical conditions.
Remove Curse	Frees object or person from curse.
Remove Disease	Cures all diseases affecting subject.
Searing Light	Ray deals 1d8/two levels, more against undead.
Secret Page	Changes one page to hide its real content.
Sepia Snake Sigil	Creates text symbol that immobilizes reader.
Shrink Item	Object shrinks to one-twelfth size.
Sleet Storm	Hampers vision and movement.
Slow	One subject/level takes only partial actions, -2 AC, -2 melee rolls.
Speak with Plants	The caster can talk to normal plants and plant creatures.
Spike Growth	Creatures in area take 1d4 damage, may be slowed.
Snare	Creates a magical booby trap.
Stinking Cloud	Nauseating vapors, 1 round/level.
Stone Shape	Sculpts stone into any form.
Suggestion	Compels subject to follow stated course of action.
Summon Monster III	Calls outsider to fight for the caster.
Summon Nature's Ally III	Calls creature to fight.
Tiny Hut	Creates shelter for 10 creatures.
Tongues	Speak any language.

Vampiric Touch	Touch deals 1d6/two caster levels; caster gains damage as hp.
Water Breathing	Subjects can breathe underwater.
Water Walk	Subject treads on water as if solid.
Wind Wall	Deflects arrows, smaller creatures, and gases.

4TH LEVEL SPELLS

Air Walk	Subject treads on air as if solid (climb at 45-degree angle).
Antiplant Shell	Keeps animated plants at bay.
Arcane Eye	Invisible floating eye moves 30 ft./round.
Bestow Curse	-6 to an ability; -4 on attacks, saves, and checks; or 50% chance of losing each action.
Black Tentacles	1d4 +1/level tentacles grapple randomly within 15 ft.
Charm Monster	Makes monster believe it is the caster's ally.
Confusion	Makes subject behave oddly for 1 round/level.
Contagion	Infects subject with chosen disease.
Control Water	Raises or lowers bodies of water.
Cure Critical Wounds	Cures 4d8 +1/level damage (max +20).
Death Ward	Grants immunity to death spells and effects.
Detect Scrying	Alerts the caster of magical eavesdropping.
Dimensional Anchor	Bars extradimensional movement.
Discern Lies	Reveals deliberate falsehoods.
Dimensional Anchor	Bars extradimensional movement.
Dismissal	Forces a creature to return to the Navirim
Divination	Provides useful advice for specific proposed actions.
Dispel Magic	Cancels magical spells and effects.
Emotion	Arouses strong emotion in subject.
Enervation	Subject gains 1d4 negative levels.
Fear	Subjects within cone flee for 1 round/level.
Fire Shield	Creatures attacking the caster take fire damage; the caster is protected from heat or cold.
Fire Trap	Opened object deals 1d4 +1/level damage.
Flame Strike	Smites foes with divine fire (1d6/level).
Freedom of Movement	Subject moves normally despite impediments.
Giant Vermin	Turns insects into giant vermin.
Greater Magic Weapon	+1 bonus/three levels (max +5).
Hallucinatory Terrain	Makes one type of terrain appear like another (field into forest, etc.).
Ice Storm	Hail deals 5d6 damage in cylinder 40 ft. across.
Illusory Wall	Wall, floor, or ceiling looks real, but anything can pass through.
Imbue with Spell Ability	Transfer spells to subject.
Improved Invisibility	As invisibility, but subject can attack and stay invisible.
Inflict Critical Wounds	Touch attack, 4d8 +1/level damage (max +20).

Lesser Geas	Commands subject of 7 HD or less.
Lesser Planar Ally	Exchange services with an 8 HD outsider.
Locate Creature	Indicates direction to familiar creature.
Minor Creation	Creates one cloth or wood object.
Minor Globe of Invulnerability	Stops 1st- through 3rd-level spell effects.
Mnemonic Enhancer	Prepares extra spells or retains one just cast. Wizard only.
Neutralize Poison	Detoxifies venom in or on subject.
Phantasmal Killer	Fearsome illusion kills subject or deals 3d6 damage.
Poison	Touch deals 1d10 Con damage, repeats in 1 min.
Polymorph Other	Gives one subject a new form.
Polymorph Self	The caster assumes a new form.
Quench	Extinguishes nonmagical fires or one magic item.
Rainbow Pattern	Lights prevent 24 HD of creatures from attacking or moving away.
Repel Vermin	Insects stay 10 ft. away.
Remove Curse	Frees object or person from curse.
Resilient Sphere	Force globe protects but traps one subject.
Restoration	Restores level and ability score drains.
Rusting Grasp	The caster's touch corrodes iron and alloys.
Scrying	Spies on subject from a distance.
Sending	Delivers short message anywhere, instantly.
Shadow Conjuration	Mimics conjuring below 4th level.
Shout	Deafens all within cone and deals 2d6 damage.
Sleet Storm	Hampers vision and movement.
Solid Fog	Blocks vision and slows movement.
Spell Immunity	Subject is immune to one spell/four levels.
Spike Stones	Creatures in area take 1d8 damage, may be slowed.
Status	Monitors condition, position of allies.
Stoneskin	Stops blows, cuts, stabs, and slashes.
Summon Monster IV	Calls outsider to fight for the caster.
Tongues	Speak any language.
Wall of Fire	Deals 2d4 fire damage out to 10 ft. and 1d4 out to 20 ft. Passing through wall deals 2d6 +1/level.
Wall of Ice	Ice plane creates wall with 15 hp +3/level, or hemisphere can trap creatures inside.

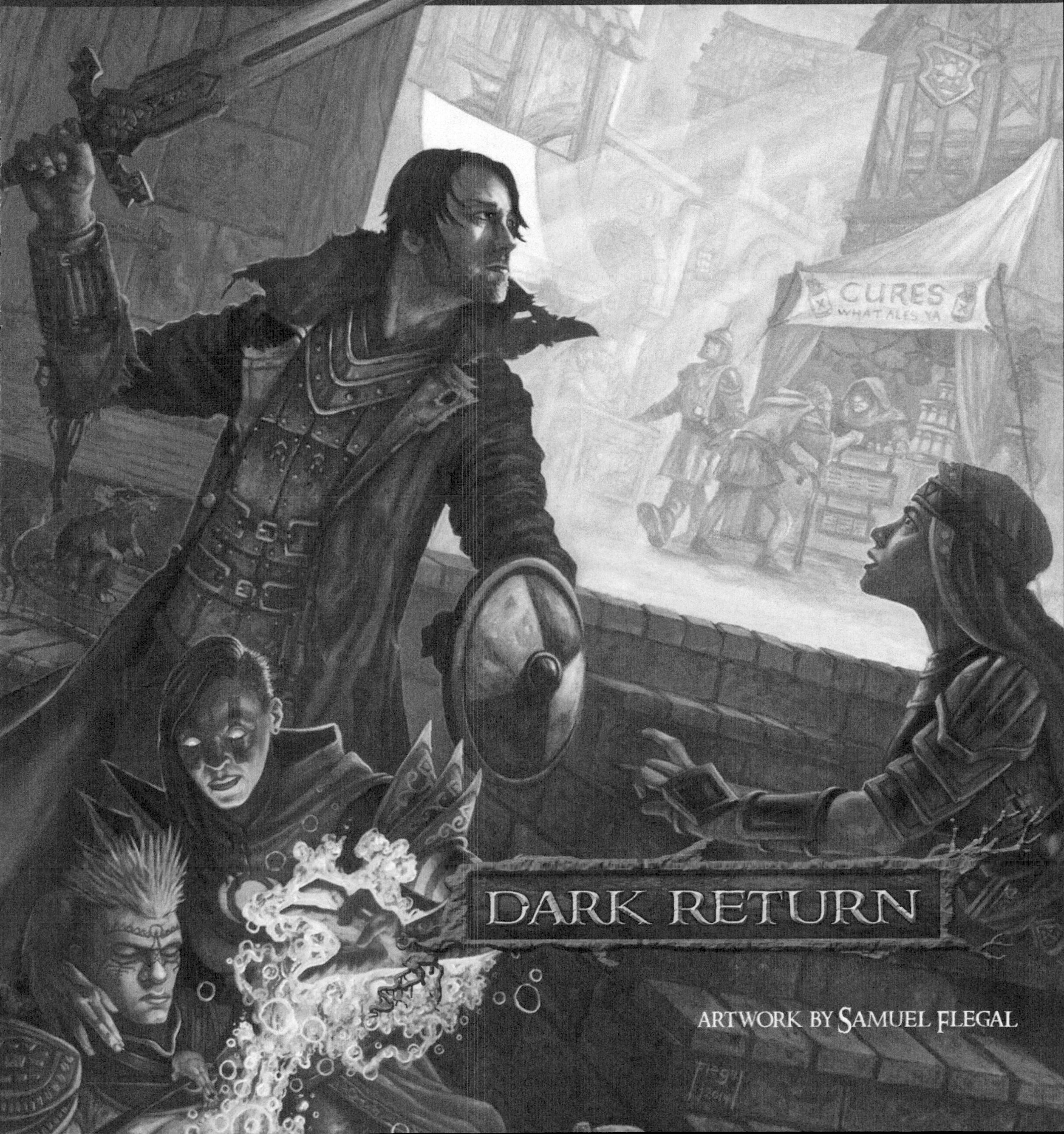
CURES
WHAT ALES YA
DARK RETURN
ARTWORK BY SAMUEL FLEGAL

CPSIA information can be obtained
at www.ICGtesting.com
Printed in the USA
FSOW03n0609060717
35766FS